Fiesta in Mexico means dancing, markets aglow with mountains of fruit and displays of handicrafts, fireworks popping during the day and lighting the evening sky with brilliance. Fiestas are banners flying from cantinas, masses and processions.

Fiesta is also taken quite literally in Mexico to mean 'feast.'

And feast you will when you prepare and serve the wonderful foods in this refreshingly different cookbook. The authors have searched the whole of Mexico to find national and regional recipes that will honor every table and enchant every taste. They have included an index of foreign food names as well as an English index and a selected list of *Things to Know* about Mexican cookery, making their book a valuable, easy-to-use addition to anyone's library of favorite recipes.

RUTH WATT MULVEY
and LUISA MARIA ALVAREZ

GOOD

FROM

New, Revised Edition

FOOD
MEXICO

COLLIER BOOKS
NEW YORK, N.Y.

Library of Congress Catalog Card Number: 62-21175

Contents

Good Food From Mexico

"Joy and Fiesta and Ritual"

FOOD IS JOY and fiesta and ritual in Mexico. When a child is baptized, hosts of friends and relatives make the pilgrimage to the church. And, with no less solemnity return with the Named One to the home where the long christening fiesta table glows in the patio.

Feasting marks the cycle of life from birth to death.

All through the November day, you will see the tireless processions of men and children, women wearing their face-shadowing rebozos, winding their way to the cemeteries where their dead lie under the hot Mexican sun. In their arms are the brilliant calendulas and the marigold-like blossoms the Aztecs named zempoal xochitl—"death flower"—which will brighten the graves of their departed. In their hands are the lovingly created luncheons and dinners, the wrapped delicacies and the clay jugs of pulque to share with the dead.

For death is no hostile stranger to these people who believe in after life. And, of course, food is important to the dead. Is it not the most important thing in life?

In Mexico, it is.

In Mexico, food is poetry. It is high romance and mundane work. It is the expression of affection. It is blessings shared.

Even in the most cosmopolitan of cities there is nothing unfamiliar about the knock at the door which precedes the proffered dish of tamales or dessert. "It turned out so well," is the gracious explanation. Although Christmas means only family and friends in private gathering around the midnight table on the Noche Buena, all of the housewives present each other with some delicacy of the season: usually buñuelos, the wafer-thin sweet pancakes.

Not long ago, a friend remembering Mexican Christmases past, sighed as she related how for five days the house had been kept in a flurry and the girls busy making dozens and dozens of the ethereal pastries; patting the dough of flour, salt, egg and water into the thinnest of pancakes, frying them in bubbling fat and dipping them in sugar syrup.

"This batch for Tomasita. This batch for Rosario," our friend re-echoed wistfully.

Food has always been more than mere subsistence, even to the poorest Indians of the country. When the Spanish Conquistadores landed in 1519, they were given presents of gold and silver and jewels so priceless that they enslaved an entire empire to gain the source. Chiefest honor, however, was the special dishes which had been prepared by the Aztecs for the "visitors."

Through the centuries Mexicans have continued to share bread with friends and with honored guests. Indeed, the national dish—the famous Mole de Guajolote—was created in the spirit of the Legion of Merit.

More than three centuries ago, word came to the nuns living in a convent in the quiet tiled city of Puebla that the Viceroy would visit their institution on his next trip. Like women the world over, they began to worry about household matters.

Would the Viceroy be comfortable? Would he approve of the management of the convent? What could they do to entertain him?

The Mother Superior called a hurried conference to discuss the matter with the members of the Order.

A play, perhaps? A concert? Recitations, then? They could dramatize a selection from the Bible?

No. No. No. They were voted down one by one. Not special enough.

At length one of the nuns spoke up. The best thing for any man, viceroy or not, she said sensibly, would be the delight of an excellent dinner. But, what? Flushed by the first triumph of her approved suggestion, the little nameless nun thought that it should be something truly extraordinary. Heads nodded a second time. What could be more unusual and more appropriate than a variation of the principal fiesta dish of the Aztecs?

So. . . .

The imaginative realist who had proposed the idea of an excellent meal was elected to fashion the Viceroy's dinner. However, all the rest promised a helping hand to the cook. Contrary to proverbial wisdom, it was the helping hands that turned the trick and the too many cooks who were responsible for giving Mexico its most familiar and most beloved dish.

First, several of the largest turkeys that could be found in the market were cut up and the carcasses, necks, legs and other appendages put into a kettle and boiled. The breasts and large chunks of meat were fried in one of the enormous clay cazuelas or crocks made by the townsmen and ground tomatoes and chilies were added. Then, some of the broth was taken from the kettle and it was allowed to simmer. "Sesame seed. Garlic. Onion. Almonds. Tortillas," helpful voices urged.

And, helpful hands poured: Cloves. Blackpepper. Aniseed. Salt. Chocolate. Raisins. Cinnamon. A little of everything on the shelves of the convent kitchen followed fast.

Thus the Mole Poblano was born.

The Viceroy proclaimed his dignified approval. The approval of the rest of Mexico is signified on every menu in the Republic where the mole poblano (Puebla mole) is still the most respected of offerings. It is found on every christening table; at every marriage feast. It is part of every festive occasion in the country. And, it is also the pièce de résistance of funeral meals.

Curiously enough Puebla, like the nuns who gave the dish to Mexico, is purely Spanish. Mole, itself, like most of the other dishes in this book are of native origin. The tortillas, for example, the staple of the Mexican diet, are still prepared in the same fashion as when the Indian tribes dominated the western continent. And archaeological discoveries show that not the slightest change has been made since earliest times.

Although every Mexican newspaper carries persuasive advertisements about the new tortilla mills, which will manufacture "at least one thousand an hour," the people still cling to the old way of grinding corn on the porous rock metates or grinding stones. The corn is slightly cooked and soaked overnight in lime water, then ground on the metate into a paste and patted into thin pancakes, after which it is cooked on top of a charcoal stove.

Like the incessant drums which dramatize Haitian life, like the ever-present cacophony of horns in a city symphony, all Mexico is in the rhythm set by the sound of hands patting tortillas.

The main source of life in Mexico, tortillas serve a multitude of purposes and are infinitely disguised. A taco is a tortilla wrapped around beans, meat, or cheese and eggs, and seasoned with chili. Enchiladas are tortillas wrapped around sliced chicken or shredded meat, seasoned with onion, chili, and garlic and fried and served hot with a highly seasoned sauce poured over them. Quesadillas are turnovers made of tortillas filled with cheese, potatoes or squash flowers.

Everywhere you will find street vendors dispensing tortillas in one form or another. Even in the most fashionable restaurants and the wealthiest homes, tortillas are an ever-present must; this, despite the fact that in Mexico City alone there are more than sixty different varieties of bread; each with a special name.

While everyone eats tortillas, three-fourths of the "other half" of the nation survive on them. The diet of two-thirds of Mexico's forty million inhabitants consists entirely of frijoles or beans, tortillas, chili and pulque. Health food addicts may marvel, but it is no mystery to the nutritionist that the people continue to flourish, for all these foods are incredibly rich in vitamins and minerals. The daily quotient of Vitamin A is contained in only six grams of chili. Pulque, on which babies are sometimes weaned, has such a high content of Vitamin B in addition to Vitamins A and C that it is often prescribed by specialists in cases of acute anemia.

Like tortillas, tamales are eaten everywhere in Mexico, although they vary from place to place. Considered an antojito, which is from the Spanish verb meaning "to feel a capricious desire for," tamales are more substantial than whimsical. They consist of corn meal mixed with meat or chili and occasionally herbs, wrapped in corn husks or in banana leaves (in the South) and steamed. Tamales are eaten for breakfast, for supper, but never at lunch.

For lunch, as you know, is the main meal in Mexico. The evening meal is consequently sketchy and usually consists of little more than sweet bread or tamales with coffee, atole (a hot drink made of corn, milk, sugar and flavoring), and chocolate.

Chocolate, or cacahuatl as it was originally called, is one of Mexico's gifts to the world.

It proved so popular in Europe after the return of the Spaniards that one of the popes forbade its use on the grounds that it was an aphrodisiac. Legend has it that the supreme epicure Moctezuma was the first to discover chocolate ice and sent his runners to the heights of the volcano to bring back blocks of snow over which thick chocolate was poured, whipped, and served as chilled froth. A rare morning treat, Mexican chocolate is different from chocolate drunk anywhere in the world. Part of its unique flavor comes from the admixture of cinnamon and vanilla.

Despite the invasion of bottled soft drinks from the States, the native beverages continue to be popular. Pulque, which tastes something like a yeast cake dissolved in lukewarm water, reigns supreme. It has since 1045 when Topiltzin Quetzalcoatl was so entranced with the "honey water" discovered by sixteen-year-old Xoxhitl that he married her. To the princess, whose name means Flower, is given credit for bringing to the Mexican good earth what was once considered a ceremonial drink and the special property of the goddess with four hundred sons.

Like mezcal and tequila, pulque comes from the maguey cactus plant and is only partially fermented. No native celebration is complete without it and the Indians, particularly those living in communities without adequate water supply systems, drink astonishing quantities of it: as many as twenty-five or thirty quarts on a single busy day.

More important to Mexican city life is coffee—which found in Mexico and other Latin American countries a natural habitat after the first plants were brought to Brazil in 1754 by a Franciscan monk.

Nearly every street in the capital and most of the other large towns has its café. And it is in these cafés that the commercial, social and political destinies of Mexico are determined. Much like the coffee shops of Europe and England in the eighteenth century, the cafés of Mexico are dedicated to philosophizing. For hours on any busy week day afternoon at the Papagayo, at Chufas, at the Café Paris Express, groups of Mexico City men sit over their tiny cups of café solos or glasses of hot milk flavored and colored with thick coffee syrup, determining which group shall have political power, what laws shall be enacted, what financial transactions consummated. Or even who shall win this next game of dominoes. As characteristically Mexican as the tortillas and the coffee habit and the siesta is the barbecue. Not the barbecue as we know it from the roadside in the United States or the tablespoons of chopped meat and tomato sauce on rolls at the drive-ins, but genuine old-world feasts accomplished on Sundays and holidays around the vast open air pits where burning maguey spikes impart a subtle and delicious flavor to the mutton, lamb, kids or beeves being roasted. Barbacoa-Domingos signs dot the highway.

And barbecue in its Sunday best it is, with children playing about in the fields and their elders rolling gently in their chairs, their eyes glazed with pulque and fresh cooked meat.

One of the chief delicacies in Mexico is fish. It is served in a thousand different ways: raw, smoked, baked, stuffed, boiled, pickled, broiled over open fires or fried lovingly. Fish was so favored by one of the last of the Aztec emperors that he had a special contingent of runners, 300 of them, whose sole duty it was to carry up the steep slopes to Mexico City fresh fish from Veracruz, some 454 kilometers away.

Today, the process is reversed. Residents of Mexico City make pilgrimages to the seaport town to sit in the portales which surround the square and eat themselves into fantastic dreams. Waiters, holding in their left hands huge plates of sea food, rush out of the hotels and restaurants with foaming tarros of the draft beer, which pours down from the mountain region around the Pico de Orizaba.

Although fish is not a regional affair, since every lake and river in the country is amply stocked with the nitrogen-rich Charal, everyone in Mexico at one time or another makes a gustatory pilgrimage to the Veracruzana fish shrine to taste the wonderful squid cooked in its "black ink" or to eat octopus, or filet of sole that is something new under the sun to everyone who has ever confused it with flounder. Shrimps, lobster, crabs, barnacles, tiny live clams, shark and a host of other treasures of the sea all have their properly rewarded and rewarding ends on the bare boards of the tables of Veracruz.

Many go to San Luis Potosi in the North for a wonderful dessert made of concentrated cactus fruit. Of the size and consistency of a soap bar, this delicious queso de tuna is at its best when eaten with a glass of ice-cold milk. In San Luis, too, you will find the wonderful mutton dish called Chito, which is peculiar to the regional fiestas and which we have encountered nowhere else in the world.

Through the country to Yucatan, where the specialty is a yellowish chicken pie called Movipollo, Mexican states vie with each other in cuisine. Everywhere, there is a great show about serving the regional dishes and everywhere a small appetite is considered a mark of unfriendliness. But even an experienced trencherman would find it difficult to work his way through a formal Mexican meal. Particularly when the soup is pozole which boasts three kinds of meat.

Pozole, another national dish, involves two days of preparation at the least. On the first day, ground corn is put into lime water and boiled slowly to separate the chaff. On the morning of the second day, the water is drained off and the corn is put into a large clay pan with a pig's head and feet, chunks of pork and chicken. Only the pig's feet have been previously cooked. When the meat is half cooked and the corn kernels have begun to boil, salt is added and chili and garlic.

After several hours more of slow cooking the mixture is ladled into soup plates, which are surrounded by side dishes of lettuce, fresh cheese, radishes, tortillas and herbs.

This is but prelude to the meal.

From soup the natural progression is to the various nuts, fruits and delicacies which constitute the dessert course.

Until 1926, when President Calles closed the churches and religious houses, the convents were the main source of sweets in Mexico, and some of them gained national fame for certain delicacies. The nuns in Guanajuato made tiny and exquisitely colored fruits from almond paste. The convent of Santa Clara in Puebla specialized in camotes de

Santa Clara, which are still sold in that city. They are composed of sweet potatoes boiled in sugar syrup, molded into candle shapes and adorned with tiny sugar flowers. The nuns of the convents of Queretaro specialized in turrones, candies made of almond paste.

Everywhere you will find a passion for sweets expressed in interesting ways in this country where even the tiniest baby clutches at his small piece of sugar cane. Perhaps no sight is more characteristically Mexican than the candy vendor, balancing on his head an enormous tray of dulces outside the church doors on Sunday morning or in parks along the city streets. In Mexico City, near the dusty old plaza named Ampudia is the sweet-smelling colorful candy mart where three hundred and more families make their living by manufacturing and selling varieties of candy.

This is the story of what is eaten in Mexico, but the eating itself is even more memorable.

Forever you will recall the broad-boned faces, shadowed by the light of tiny charcoal burners, as the vendors squat over the piles of roasting chestnuts that fill the air with fragrance on a winter evening. Forever you will recall the end of the night baseball game and surging out with the crowd of fanaticos to sit at one of the benches before a stall selling chicken soup. You will remember the blaze of noon at Tres Cumbres on the road to Cuernavaca with the cars lined up before the tacos stands.

You will remember too the ornate mahogany of the Opera Bar and holiday evenings when you ate sweet rice and an infinite variety of sea food on the roof of the Majestic Hotel, which overlooks the zocalo and the great cathedral.

The memory of food will be the memory of Mexico.

Chapter 1

Appetizers, Cocktails and Beverages

THE SPANIARDS brought with them domesticated meats, baked foods, desserts and candies and a whole cuisine that was quickly incorporated into the national diet. In the nineteenth century the French dream of New World conquest arrived in the persons of the Austrian Archduke Maximilian and his lovely Belgian wife. They introduced the charm and subtlety of European court life and the artistry of French royal kitchens.

Later the United States "discovered" Mexico. It was an enchanted moment and soon the early expeditionists hunting gold were followed by other North Americans hunting a place in the sun where life was easy and full of charm and the ultimate freedom to relax and enjoy it.

Mexico was equally enchanted. Among other things, the people from the North brought with them the coctel and no society column of a metropolitan paper is complete without at least three chronicles of cocteles the day before.

But as with Spanish, French, Italian and Austrian contributions, the Mexicans adapted the cocktail party to their own needs, arts and abilities. In Mexico it is more of an eating event than in the United States. Usually it begins at seven in the evening, when the satisfaction of the heavy noon meal has worn off, and continues until nine-thirty or ten o'clock when it is time for the late supper.

Naturally food is as important as the Scotch or tequila.

The idea of canapés therefore is somewhat more substantial than in the United States, but the Mexicanized type has become so popular that in this country, and now in the United States, they are favorite fare—hearty, spicy and small, yet adequate conversation pieces. Very quickly the tortilla became essential. It is served plain and toasted, fried in deep fat or in a bewildering variety of combinations. Small tortillas are spread with avocado paste; covered with frijoles; are heaped with salad and shredded meat and cheese and livened with Mexican sauces.

As a matter of pleasurable fact, all of the favorite anto-jitos in miniature have become cocktail tidbits. Tamales, hot and the size of a little finger, are tempting and an invitation to have another bite. Tortas are concocted of infinitesimal rolls stuffed with the favorite chorizo or pâté combined with frijoles, lettuce, chili and avocado.

To lend spice to a coctel, hostesses take canned chilies jalapeños, remove the skin, stem and seeds, and stuff them with cream cheese combined with nuts. After several hours in the refrigerator, they are sliced very thin for an exciting canapé. So popular has cocktail food become that the buffet is even more important than the bar.

A number of hosts, nationals and visitors, have seized upon the "tipic." Mariachis, a marimba band or a guitar player have become part of the cocktail scene. Parties are held in patios where Indian women in regional dress sit beneath the orange trees and concoct at their charcoal braziers hot tacos in miniature or fashion delicate chalupas of tortilla dough in the form of little canoes filled with chicken, pork, veal or sausage fried with tomatoes and onions and garnished with a little chili or some green chili sauce.

Shrimp is also popular and because it is plentiful, it is served more frequently and in a wider variety of ways than in the United States. The huge shrimp from Campeche are served whole. They also come fried, pickled or plain with accompanying chili sauce or with a rich avocado sauce livened with chili.

But, perhaps the most popular of all tidbits are pepitas— tiny green roasted squash seeds. In homes as well as in bars, pepitas inevitably come with cocktails. They are prepared by soaking squash seeds in water with charcoal ash for half a day until the outer husks are easily removed. The small kernels are then toasted with butter and salt.

You guests may be able to take liquor or leave it alone, but not your Mexican canapés.

CANAPÉS DE AGUACATE (*Avocado Canapés*)

4 avocados
1 teaspoon salt
⅛ teaspoon pepper
1 tablespoon lemon juice

2 cooked chicken breasts,
  chopped
¼ cup mayonnaise
12 slices white bread

Pit avocados, peel and mash. Add salt, pepper, lemon juice, chicken breasts and mayonnaise, and blend. Remove crusts from bread, halve and spread with avocado mixture. Yield: twenty-four canapés.

CANASTAS (*Basket Canapés*)

12 whole-wheat biscuits
1 cup fat
1 small can black caviar

2 canned pimientos
Parsley

Cut the biscuits in half and scoop out the center to form little bowls. Fry the outsides in fat and drain well. Spread center with black caviar and fashion a tiny flower of pimiento for the center of each canapé. Make leaves and stems from parsley. Yield: twenty-four canapés.

CANAPÉ NACIONAL (*National Canapé*)

12 slices bread
1 small can pâté de foie gras

3 small raw green peppers
1 small can salmon caviar

Cut the bread into thin strips, toast and spread with pâté. Peel peppers, seed, and cut into tiny oval shapes, like cactus leaves, and into long thin strips for stems. Place a leaf with stem on each slice of toast and surround with the caviar to resemble the cactus fruit. Yield: three dozen canapés.

OSTIONES DE GUAYMAS (*Oysters, Guaymas-Style*)

3 dozen large fresh oysters
2 tablespoons lemon juice
1½ tablespoons salt
4 onions, chopped fine
½ cup olive oil
1 cup vinegar

1 teaspoon allspice
1 teaspoon pepper
3 cloves garlic, broiled and
 chopped
1 canned chili Jalapeño, cut
 into strips (Page 238).

Shuck oysters and put them in a pot with one cup water, lemon juice and one tablespoon salt and simmer about five minutes. Soak onions in one and one-half cups of boiling water with one teaspoon salt for five minutes. Drain and fry in oil two or three minutes. Add to oysters. Add vinegar, allspice, pepper, garlic, chili and one tablespoon juice from canned chilies. Cover the bowl and let stand for twenty-four hours. Yield: six to eight servings.

ESCABECHE CAMPECHANO (*Pickled Fish, Campeche-Style*)

2 pounds sliced fish
Juice of one lime
2 tablespoons salt
1 tablespoon chili powder
½ cup vinegar
3 large onions, sliced thick

1 cup olive oil
5 cloves garlic
10 black peppercorns
½ teaspoon orégano
½ teaspoon laurel
1 teaspoon allspice

Wash the fish slices and soak ten minutes in enough water to cover with the juice of the lime and one tablespoon of salt. Dissolve the chili powder and one teaspoon salt in the vinegar. Soak the onions in boiling water to which one teaspoon of salt has been added, drain and soak in the vinegar for fifteen minutes. Remove, reserving onions and vinegar.

Heat olive oil and fry two whole cloves of garlic until they are browned. Discard garlic. Add fish, peppercorns, orégano, laurel, allspice, the rest of the garlic, chopped, and reserved vinegar. Do not add water. Simmer over low heat fifteen minutes. Serve cold, garnished with onion slices. Yield: six servings.

CAMARONES EN FRIO I (*Pickled Shrimp I*)

1½ pounds fresh shrimp
2 cloves garlic, chopped
3 onions
¾ cup olive oil
⅓ cup vinegar

Salt, mustard and pepper to
taste
⅓ can, or less, chilies
Jalapeños (Page 238)
2 tomatoes, sliced

Wash shrimp, peel and clean. Fry the garlic and one chopped onion in one-quarter cup oil until brown, add the shrimp and fry for about ten minutes. Cool and cover with the following sauce:

Mix vinegar with one-half cup olive oil; season with salt, mustard, pepper, chilies and liquid from the can. Place the shrimp on a platter, cover with sauce and garnish with tomatoes and slices of the other onions which have been soaked in salt water for a few hours. Yield: six servings.

CAMARONES EN FRIO II (*Pickled Shrimp II*)

2 onions
4 cloves garlic
1 tablespoon butter or
margarine
1 pound fresh shrimp,
boiled, peeled
2 medium-sized tomatoes, or
1 cup canned tomatoes

1 canned chili Jalapeño
with liquid (Page 238)
¼ cup vinegar
½ cup olive oil
Salt, pepper and mustard

Chop one onion and the garlic and sauté in butter or margarine until a golden brown. Add shrimp, tomatoes which have been peeled and chopped, and fry together about ten minutes. Cool. Mix one-quarter cup chili liquid, vinegar and olive oil. Season to taste wth salt, pepper and mustard and pour over the shrimp mixture. Allow to marinate in the refrigerator for several hours or even overnight. Before serving, garnish with slices of the other onion which has been soaked in salt water for two hours. Yield: six servings.

TORTITAS COMPUESTAS (*Tiny Rolls, Garnished*)

12 tiny rolls
1½ cups Mexican Refried
   Beans (Page 149).
1 cup shredded lettuce
1 tablespoon French
   dressing
¾ cup shredded cooked
   chicken
Salmon or sardines
1 small avocado, sliced
Chili

Split rolls and reserve tops. Remove inside crumb of rolls and fill with bean paste, lettuce which has been marinated with French dressing, chicken or fish and avocado. Add chili to taste and cover with reserved tops of rolls. Serve cold. Yield: twelve canapés.

TORTILLAS ENROLLADAS (*Tortilla Rolls*)

2 hard-cooked eggs, chopped
1 sweet green or red pepper,
   chopped
¼ cup cream cheese
1 teaspoon grated onion
1 teaspoon salt
6 tortillas (*bought*)
Fat for deep frying

Mix together eggs, pepper, cream cheese, onion and salt. Cut tortillas in half and spread with egg-pepper mixture. Roll and fasten with picks. Fry in deep hot fat (360 degrees F.) till brown. Yield: twelve canapés.

TORTILLAS TOSTADAS (*Toasted Tortillas*)

Dissolve one tablespoon salt in one-half cup water and sprinkle tortillas well. Cut into small squares or wedges and let stand ten minutes or till almost dry. Fry in deep hot fat (360 degrees F.) till brown. Use as base for the following canapés:

ACEITUNAS (olive) CANAPÉS: Spread toasted tortilla squares with chopped stuffed olives and garnish with grated cheese.

FRIJOLES (beans) CANAPÉS: Put a teaspoon of Mexican fried beans (Page 149) on a toasted tortilla square and garnish with a slice of cream cheese.

GUACAMOLE (avocado) CANAPÉS: Put a teaspoon of Guacamole (Page 59) on each toasted tortilla square.

JICARA (black caviar) CANAPÉS: Spread toasted tortilla squares with black caviar and decorate with pieces of pimiento, hard-cooked eggs and green pepper.

TOTOPOS (cream cheese) CANAPÉS: Spread toasted tortilla wedges with cream cheese which has been blended with chopped green pepper and salt and pepper to taste.

COCKTAILS

COCTEL CUERNAVACA (*Cuernavaca Cocktail*)

⅓ part rum   ⅓ part French vermouth
⅓ part Italian vermouth   Crushed ice

Mix all ingredients in cocktail shaker and shake well.

COCTEL ALEGRIA (*Happiness Cocktail*)

6 jiggers of brandy   1 tablespoon powdered
1 sprig of mint, chopped   cinnamon
Rinds of two lemons, grated   1 jigger cointreau
6 black peppers, finely   3 jiggers port wine
  ground   3 tablespoons sugar
6 cloves, ground   Crushed ice

Mix the first six ingredients and let stand in a covered container for five or six hours. Before serving add cointreau, port, sugar and ice. Mix well and serve very cold. Yield: six servings.

COCTEL DE MANGO (*Mango Cocktail*)

2 mangoes
Crushed ice
3 jiggers gin
4 teaspoons sugar

1 egg
½ teaspoon nutmeg
6 cherries

Peel mangoes, mash pulp and pass through a sieve. Put in cocktail shaker with ice, gin, sugar, egg and nutmeg and shake well. Serve with cherries. Yield: six cocktails.

COCTEL AMIGO (*Friend Cocktail*)

1 jigger tequila
1 jigger French vermouth
1 jigger crème de menthe
2 teaspoons lemon or lime
   juice

1 teaspoon sugar
Crushed ice

Mix all ingredients in a cocktail shaker and shake well. Yield: two servings.

COCTEL FRONTERA (*Frontier Cocktail*)

1 jigger tequila
1 jigger vermouth
½ jigger grenadine

1 teaspoon orange juice
1 teaspoon lemon juice
Chopped ice

Mix all ingredients in cocktail shaker and shake well. Yield: two servings.

COCTEL INDIO (*Indian Cocktail*)

4 tablespoons rum
4 tablespoons pineapple
   juice

2 tablespoons anisette
1 tablespoon raspberry syrup

Mix well, add crushed ice and enough soda to fill two glasses. Stir. Yield: two cocktails.

COCTEL DE PIÑA (*Pineapple Cocktail*)

1 part tequila
1 part habanero

1 part vermouth
½ part pineapple juice

Shake with crushed ice and serve very cold.

RON COPITA (*Rum Drink*)

1 jigger rum
1 jigger anisette
1 teaspoon sugar

1 teaspoon lime juice
Crushed ice

Mix all ingredients in cocktail shaker and shake well. Yield: one serving.

RON COCTEL (*Rum Cocktail*)

1 cup rum
2 tablespoons lemon juice
2 tablespoons sugar

Few drops crème de menthe
Crushed ice
1 cup sparkling water

Mix ingredients in cocktail shaker and shake well. Yield: six servings.

COCTEL TEQUILA DORADA (*Golden Tequila Cocktail*)

1 part tequila   ½ part lemon juice
1 part honey   Crushed ice

Mix ingredients in cocktail shaker and shake well.

TEQUILA ALTA (*Tall Tequila*)

1 jigger tequila   Tonic
1 teaspoon lime juice

Pour tequila over ice cubes in a tall glass. Add lime juice and fill with Tonic.

COCTEL TEQUILA I (*Tequila Cocktail I*)

¼ cup syrup   Few drops vanilla
¼ cup tequila   Crushed ice
⅓ cup vermouth

Mix all ingredients in cocktail shaker and shake well. Yield: four servings.

COCTEL TEQUILA II (*Tequila Cocktail II*)

1 part tequila   Crushed ice
1 part lemon juice
1 teaspoon sugar per jigger
  of tequila

Mix ingredients in cocktail shaker and shake well.

PLATA TASQUEÑA (*Taxco Silver Cocktail*)

2 jiggers tequila	Crushed ice
1 teaspoon sugar	Soda water
1 egg white	
½ tablespoon lemon or lime juice	

Shake together all ingredients except soda water. Serve in a highball glass with soda water. Yield: one serving.

COCTEL VERACRUZANA (*Veracruz Cocktail*)

⅓ part pineapple juice	⅓ part French vermouth
⅓ part rum	Cracked ice

Mix ingredients in cocktail shaker and shake well.

SEVICHE DE ACAPULCO (*Acapulco Fish Cocktail*)

1 pound fish, preferably pompano or sierra (or use oysters, lobster or crab)	1 teaspoon pepper
	½ teaspoon orégano
	2 tablespoons vinegar
¾ cup lemon juice	2 medium-sized tomatoes, chopped
1 large onion, chopped	¼ cup olive oil
1 canned chili verde, chopped (Page 238)	

Remove bones from fish. Shred meat and place in china or earthenware dish and cover with lemon juice. Let stand one hour. Drain and wash in cold water. Mix remaining ingredients except oil, blend with fish, then add oil. Serve cold in cocktail glasses. Yield: six servings.

BEVERAGES

When the ambassadors of Cortes encountered the Aztec Emperor Moctezuma, he was at the breakfast table shielded by a rich screen. Servants were filing by in endless procession with tempting delicacies. The most frequent offering was a steaming aromatic drink which was called cacahuatl, meaning sour water. The thin beverage made from water and seeds, so valuable that they were used as currency in many parts of Mexico and so costly that only royalty could afford them, was a favorite drink.

On first taste, the Spaniards were not impressed, but when they were served the beverage sweetened with honey and flavored with spices and vanilla, they succumbed. In short order the chocolate habit spread to Europe. There it became inordinately popular. So popular, in fact that ecclesiastical authorities frowned upon chocolate drinking as immoral and provocative of immorality; finally a Papal Bull was issued prohibiting the faithful from drinking it.

However, frowns availed little, and even today the custom of taking chocolate is widespread. Mexican chocolate is not something found upon a shelf with simple instructions to "add one cup of water." It is still prepared with the lovely carved whirling molinillos. These whip into a steaming froth the small cinnamon-flavored cakes, which are melted in hot water and often enriched with an egg.

Even more popular is the beverage which was brought from the Old World to the New and which became a part of the national economy and national tradition of Latin American countries. Coffee is taken in two ways: with milk or boiled to a thick black syrup and served in minute "express" cups.

No Mexican breakfast or merienda is complete without café con leche. This is made by filling a glass with boiling milk and infusing it with a trifle of thick, black coffee syrup. In the afternoons at the cafés where men discuss philosophy, business and the romance of the moment, it is the small cups of black coffee which are enjoyed.

Chocolate and coffee by no means limit the list of favorite drinks. Not even the refrescos of the United States have succeeded in supplanting sidra, the fizzing apple cider; or champurrado, the corn gruel mixed with chocolate. Atole, which is also a corn gruel of various flavors, is another muy Mexicana treat and is always served with tamales. One of the most delicious experiences in the world is to stand in the market of the lovely garden city of Uruapan and drink a cup of Uruapan atole while trying to select one of the lacquered trays for which the region is famous.

Every city street has its contingent of stands or small shops with long rows of glass barrels, whose contents glow in the vivid colors of Mexican ades—strawberry, pineapple, mango, orange, tuna (the Mexican prickly pear), lime and even coconut. Prohibition has been suggested in Mexico, but no one in the final run has braved the natural way of things —which is drinking.

Mexico's national drink today, as it was when the Spaniards arrived, is pulque—the fermenting honey water of the maguey plant. No one is quite certain why it had not come about sooner, but one day in the eleventh century, a lovely young girl whose name was Flower, Xochitl, discovered that a sweet aromatic liquid could be distilled from the metl plants in the garden. Quite properly, her father brought it to his relative, the eighth Toltec king, Ce Acatl Topiltzin Quetzalcoatl, the legendary god-ruler symbolized, as his name indicates, by "The Plumed Serpent." It was the beginning of romance and more pedantic scholars will say the downfall of the wonderful Toltec empire.

Since then, the people of Mexico have consumed pulque as naturally as water—and often in greater quantity.

Efforts were made to curb the habit by seventeenth-century viceroys and by others who came after, but the cantinas like the *Sons of Moctezuma* and the *Florida* and *La Libertad* are still serving it endlessly in gourd bowls or in glasses. Women still go with their jugs in age-old fashion to the window to buy the home-consumption quantities and at fiestas, and on other special occasions, the streets in front of the cantinas wear proudly the red and white and green banners which mean that fresh pulque is inside.

Another very popular drink made from a variety of the

maguey is mezcal liquor, distilled from the fermented mash
of heart and leaf pulp. It is the special pride of the Oaxaca
region, where it is often sold in round, black pottery jugs,
each bearing a little sack of salt mixed with chile and
powdered maguey worm—a mixture guaranteed to maintain
perpetual thirst. Maguey haciendas devoted to the exclusive
cultivation of the plant are still flourishing in Mexico. Many
of the most extensive are in Jalisco, where tequila is a matter
of state pride and in no wise seems to have any effect on feet
treading the intricate patterns of the jarabe tapatio.

Tequila is taken there as elsewhere in Mexico in the simple manner of drinking a small copita, taking a taste of the
piece of lime at hand and finally a lick of salt. This other
national drink is also served in various ways and some of
the most potent and purely Mexican cocktails are made from
tequila with honey added and lime juice or the juice of
mangoes or other tropical fruits.

Rum, a Cuban drink, arrived at the port of Veracruz
along with Cuban people and many Cuban customs. Even
old-fashioneds are concocted of rum there with fresh pineapple sticks. On the West Coast many liquors are served
with fresh coconut milk and these tall chilled drinks are
enjoyed along the beaches of Acapulco, and frequently from
coconut shells.

There are other more or less alcoholic drinks in which
most Mexicans at some time or another indulge. Some of
the favorites are the fruit "wines," the heavy syrupy liquors
made of mango, guanabana, blackberry and other fruits, a
specialty of the Toluca region. Although you may think of
eggnog as a seasonal beverage, the Mexicans have concocted
a delicious brew with an egg base, rompope, which is more
like liqueur and is served at any time.

Wine is much consumed although not so freely as pulque
or beer. Mexican cerveza is undoubtedly the best in the
world and ranges from a thin light sparkling beer to the
heavy black Negra Modelo. Somewhere between the two is
a special Christmas beer which is served only during December.

Other apparently innocuous drinks are quite potent, too.
Even tepache, a beverage made of pineapple rind and water,

is preferred when it has fermented a little. In addition to mezcal and tequila, Mexico is also famous for the fiery brandy, *aguardiente,* with an alcoholic content no greater than that of other liquors but which seems to have a more devastating effect.

Cactus sap and water are allowed to ferment into colonche, and the fermented apple juice which is called sidra champagne is served everywhere at fiestas. It is at its best in the apple-producing region around Huejotzingo where you can sit at a wayside open-air cantina across from a sixteenth-century convent and watch the sun light up the snowy peaks of Popocatepetl, Ixtaccihuatl and menacing Orizaba.

CHAMPURRADO (*Chocolate made with Atole*)

⅓ cup nixtamalina, or 3
    tablespoons cornstarch
3 cups cold water
1 tablespoon brown sugar
1 tablespoon white sugar
1 teaspoon vanilla

2 squares Mexican
    chocolate, or
    2 ounces dark Dutch
      chocolate, grated, and
    1 teaspoon powdered
      cinnamon
2 cups milk

Blend nixtamalina (or cornstarch) with one cup water. Add the rest of the water and strain through a fine sieve. Pour into a saucepan and bring to a boil over low heat, stirring constantly. Add sugars, vanilla and chocolate, a little at a time, stirring constantly. Add milk slowly and cook until the mixture has achieved a creamy consistency. Yield: five or six servings.

CHOCOLATE MEXICANO (*Mexican Chocolate*)

2 pounds Soconusco cocoa
    beans
1 pound Caracas cocoa
    beans
½ cup almonds, blanched
    and lightly toasted
½ cup peanuts, blanched
    and toasted

1 tablespoon powdered
    cinnamon
1 pound sugar
1 teaspoon nutmeg
1 clove
1 egg
2 egg yolks

Grind all ingredients except eggs and stand near heat to warm. Add eggs and, while still warm, shape into little balls the size of an egg. Pat into pancakes and place on a board to cool. Wrap the chocolate pancakes in tissue paper and store in glass jars until needed. They keep indefinitely and each one makes four cups of chocolate.

CHOCOLATE

6 cups milk
3 ounces Mexican chocolate
    or dark Dutch type

1 teaspoon powdered
    cinnamon
3 eggs, beaten

Boil milk in the top of a deep double boiler five minutes. Remove from fire and add chocolate, mixed with the cinnamon, a little at a time, beating with molinillo or egg beater after each addition. When the chocolate is thoroughly blended, heat to the boiling point. Place over bottom of double boiler and add eggs, whipping constantly, until they are thoroughly blended and the mixture is frothing. Yield: eight servings.

ATOLE DE COCO (Coconut Atole)

4 tablespoons flour
1 pint water
1 small coconut, grated
1 quart milk

½ pound sugar
2-inch stick cinnamon
1 teaspoon vanilla

Blend flour and water. Heat, stirring, until thickened over low heat. Add coconut, coconut milk, milk, sugar and cinnamon. Simmer, stirring, ten minutes. Strain. Simmer, stirring often, five minutes longer. Add vanilla and serve very hot. Yield: about seven cups.

ATOLE DE FRESA (*Strawberry Atole*)

1½ quarts fresh strawberries	1 cup sugar
1 cup flour	1 teaspoon vanilla
1 pint water	1 cup cream
1 quart milk, scalded	Few drops red food coloring

Wash strawberries well and press through a colander or sieve to extract juice. Blend flour with water and add, while stirring, to scalded milk. Add sugar and cook, stirring constantly, until thickened, about ten minutes. Add strawberry juice, vanilla, cream and coloring. Heat, stirring, to boiling. Serve hot. Yield: two quarts.

HORCHATA (*Cantaloup Seed Drink*)

4 cups dried cantaloup seeds	1 tablespoon cinnamon
8 cups water	1 cup sugar

Wash cantaloup seeds and grind. Place the ground seeds in a colander and pour water slowly over them until only peeling of seeds is left in the colander. Add cinnamon and sugar to taste. Chill thoroughly before serving. The horchata most commonly served in Mexico is that made with cantaloup seeds, but it may be prepared with other seeds of the melon family or with almonds. Yield: eight to ten servings.

CHICHA (*Cooling Ade*)

1 small fresh pineapple	1 teaspoon cinnamon
1 pound sugar	½ teaspoon cloves
3 quarts water	¼ teaspoon nutmeg
3 limes, sliced	

Wash the pineapple thoroughly. Peel and chop the peeling; grind the pulp. Dissolve sugar in water and then add limes, the ground pulp and chopped peeling, cinnamon, cloves and nutmeg and allow the mixture to stand in a covered earthenware jug twenty-four hours or longer. Strain and serve cool. Yield: one gallon.

ATOLE DE ELOTE (Corn Atole)

1 cup corn kernels, finely ground	½ teaspoon baking soda
	2-inch stick cinnamon
1 quart milk, boiled	4 lemon or orange leaves

Mix corn with milk and add the soda, cinnamon and leaves. Cook over low heat, stirring constantly, ten minutes or until thickened. Yield: five servings.

ROMPOPE (Eggnog)

2 cups milk	1 cup aguardiente or brandy
1 cup sugar	1 teaspoon almond or
2-inch stick cinnamon	vanilla extract
6 egg yolks, well beaten	
¼ cup almonds, blanched and ground	

Bring milk to a boil over moderate heat. Remove, add sugar and cinnamon. Place over moderate heat again and boil ten minutes. Remove, strain and cool. Add egg yolks slowly, beating constantly. Then add almonds and place over low heat, stirring constantly with a wooden spoon until the mixture begins to boil. Remove and strain through a wet napkin. When it is quite cold, add the aguardiente slowly, stirring constantly. Add extract and allow it to stand in a cool place until the following day when it can be bottled. Keep rompope several weeks, before drinking. Serve in small liqueur glasses. Yield: about three and one-half cups.

PONCHE (*Punch*)

2 cups orange blossom water
⅓ cup brandy
⅓ cup rum
2 cups strong tea

2 cups of tea made with
  orange leaves
½ cup sugar
Peelings of two lemons or
  limes

Mix orange blossom water, brandy and rum in a pitcher or bowl. Then add the boiling teas and the sugar. Serve hot with a small piece of peel in each glass. Yield: six servings.

PONCHE DE ALMENDRAS (*Almond Punch*)

2 quarts milk
1 pound almonds, blanched
  and ground
1¼ cups sugar

¾ cup rum
2 tablespoons agua de
  azahar (orange-flower
  water)

Heat milk slowly till it comes to a boil. Add almonds and simmer five minutes. Cool and strain. Add sugar, rum and azahar, reheat and serve very hot. Yield: eight servings.

CHICHA DE FRUTAS (*Fruit Punch*)

1 small pineapple
1 gallon of water
2 cups sugar
10 cloves

2-inch stick cinnamon
2 apples
2 quinces
3 peaches

Wash pineapple thoroughly and remove rind. Crush the rind thoroughly and place it in a large pot with water, sugar, cloves and cinnamon. Boil fifteen minutes, cool and strain. To the strained juice add pineapple, apples, quince and peaches, all finely ground. Allow the mixture to stand overnight. Strain through a damp napkin, pressing fruit to extract all flavor. Allow to stand in an earthenware crock for five to seven days or until it ferments a little. Yield: one gallon.

PONCHE MEXICANA (*Mexican Punch*)

8 *tender green lemon leaves*	8 *cups water*
Peeling of one grapefruit	2 *cups sugar*
3-*inch stick cinnamon*	½ *pint tequila*

Boil the lemon leaves, grapefruit peel and cinnamon in water with sugar eight minutes. Remove and let stand one hour. Strain and add tequila. Bottle and store for at least two weeks before serving. Yield: two and one-half quarts.

REFRESCO COSTEÑO (*Coastal Drink*)

1 *cup water*	½ *cup brandy*
1¾ *cups sugar*	2 *cups white wine*
2-*inch stick cinnamon*	1 *can shredded pineapple*
1 *cup pineapple juice*	*Chopped ice*
1 *cup orange juice*	

Boil water, sugar and cinnamon over low heat for five minutes. Cool. Add fruit juices, which have been strained, brandy, wine, pineapple and ice. Mix thoroughly and serve in champagne glasses. Yield: one quart.

HORCHATA DE ALMENDRAS (*Almond Horchata*)

½ *pound almonds,*	2 *tablespoons orange blos-*
blanched and ground	*som water*
2 *quarts water*	2 *tablespoons kirsch*
1 *cup sugar*	

Allow the ground almonds to stand for one hour in a mixture of water and a syrup made by boiling sugar with one cup additional water. Drain by passing through a damp napkin, pressing well to extract all possible flavor from almonds. Add orange blossom water and kirsch and store in refrigerator for a day or longer. Serve very cold. Yield: two and one-half quarts.

CREMA BANDERA MEXICANA (*Mexican Flag Liqueur*)

1 part grenadine
1 part white crème de cacao

1 part green crème de menthe

Pour liqueurs carefully into a liqueur glass so that the colors, red, white and green, are kept separate.

CHICHA DE PIÑA (*Pineapple Drink*)

1 medium-sized pineapple
2 cups sugar

2 two-inch cinnamon sticks
4 quarts of water

Wash and peel pineapple. Chop the peeling and grate the pineapple. Boil sugar and cinnamon in water five minutes and cool. Add grated pineapple and chopped peeling and let stand overnight. Strain through a napkin and let the drink ferment at room temperature in a covered earthen jug. Fermentation will take about three days in hot weather and twice that time in winter. Yield: about four quarts.

TEPACHE (*Pineapple Nectar*)

2 pounds brown sugar
4 quarts of water
Cinnamon, cloves, anise, to taste
Pinch of black pepper

1 medium-sized pineapple, peeled, ground
1 banana, mashed
1 quart of beer or two yeast cakes

Boil together for five minutes brown sugar and water. Add spices and boil fifteen minutes. Cool. Add pineapple and banana and pour mixture into a large earthen crock (do not use metal). Add beer or yeast and allow to ferment twenty-four hours. Strain and cool. Yield: five quarts.

Chapter 2

Soups, Dry Soups and Sauces

SOUPS ARE AN INTEGRAL PART of a Mexican meal. Soups—plural.

Although many traditional eating habits have been simplified, not the custom of having *dry* and *wet* soup courses. Dry soup is usually made of rice or macaroni, vermicelli or even tortillas, cooked in soup stock until the moisture has been absorbed. Ordinarily, the dry soup follows immediately after the wet soup and may be considered a substitute for potatoes. Although potatoes are a New-World food, Mexicans are not fond of them and prefer, sensibly enough, to take their starch in the form of dry soup.

Most popular of the dry soups is Mexican rice, which is fried and later simmered in stock. Usually, this is served with a fried egg or with avocado or guacamole. White rice is also popular and green rice gives a touch of color to a meal.

Vermicelli and macaroni are served in a number of ways, sometimes covered with tingling sauce and sometimes with Mexican sausage to give body and flavor to the dish. Nor have tortillas been overlooked. The all-purpose corn wafers are included in the form of dry soups boiled, fried and baked and served simply or elaborated with tomatoes, cheese, chili and onion.

But it is in the endless variety of wet soups that imagination has had full sway.

Always a part of the meal, they have a completeness which make them desirable dishes at any time. Wet soups may be sturdy: like vermicelli soup, lentil soup, bean soup, corn soup or the sopa campesina. Puchero, which is listed under soups is actually a Mexican boiled dinner with a host of ingredients from twenty-three to thirty, including sweet potatoes, peaches, pears, lamb, avocados, cabbage, beef, corn, turnips and chick peas. Sometimes it is served as a meal in itself in the country.

Soups may be nothing more than water infused with flavor like the savory garlic soup. They may be romantic as squash flower soup and as exotic as hazel nuts cooked into a fluid delicacy.

Quite frequently soups are very festive. Pozole is the essential of any village celebration in small towns in Nayarit. There, and in Sonora, it is the custom for the villagers and their guests to gather in the community house or in the home of the fiesta sponsor and while some are dancing to exciting music, others chatting, the first relay of merry-makers sits down to the bowls of pozole and hot tortillas which form the fiesta dinner.

Not infrequently soups have been found the only remedy for too much fiesta. The particular cure is the mouth-singeing menudo, which is one very good reason for a Sunday-morning stop at Amecameca where soup kettles on the little stoves around the plaza are bubbling and steaming from an early hour.

That is the cure. The prevention may be taken at eleven o'clock the evening before or at three in the morning at the counters of the chicken-soup stands near the car barns in Mexico City. Everyone has a favorite among the stands where the chicken soup in steaming bowls is accompanied by bowls of fiery powdered chili and bolillos served from the scrubbed bare boards.

Soups, like other arts and crafts, are regional affairs. Toluca, which prides itself on weaving, on its fabulous market and its creamy cheese, is no less concerned with its reputation for onion soup. In this matter, Puebla has achieved a delicate Churrigueresque artistry through the combination of buttermilk and tortillas. Naturally enough, the favorite of the Baja Californians is sea turtle soup. The people of the long peninsula jutting out into the Pacific count among the riches of the sea, pearl oysters, the sea pear and the caguama with its subtle flavor. One of the vivid remembrances of the "village in the sun" is Caldo Miche made with the delicious bagre fish from Lake Chapala and redolant of wild marjoram, coriander and spices, and served with green gage plums.

From the northern grain-producing states are soups of

chick peas and cereals and from the meat-produ
like Chihuahua are extravagant soups of filete o

The coastal preference is fish soups. No civil
United States has been more bitter than that b̶ ̶ ̶ ̶ ̶ ̶t̶h̶e̶
milk-only purists of the Boston clam chowder school and
the Long Island add-tomato heretics. It was history re-
peated, however. At least a century before, the battle had
begun in Mexico and still continues enthusiastically.

Tuxpam, the tiny bougainvillaea-covered town in northern Veracruz, is the unbending milk-only faction as it has
been for time out of mind. The hearty fun-loving and
heterogenous people of the port city of Veracruz, however,
prefer tomatoes with their chowder. Clams are not the only
popular sea food for soup, however. Shrimp soup is a uni-
versal favorite and soups are made from the thousand and
one fish which are found in the Gulf waters.

All of the regional and civic differences are resolved on
two points. One is that basic stock makes a world of differ-
ence. The other, that avocado is definitely at its best served
with soup. The fruit is halved and peeled and placed in the
soup dish and the proper way to eat it is to take a bit of
avocado with a spoonful of soup. Some cooks prefer to cut
the avacado into thin slices and float them on the surface of
the soup.

SOPA DE AGUACATE (*Avocado Soup*)

4 tablespoons shortening	3 medium-sized avocados,
1 tablespoon flour	mashed
¼ cup chopped onion	⅓ cup cream
½ cup tomatoes, peeled	Green food coloring
and drained	3 tortillas (bought), or
Salt and pepper	3 slices of bread
4 cups stock	

Heat one tablespoon shortening, blend in flour and brown.
Add onion and tomatoes and boil until mixture is reduced
to about one-half. Add a pinch of salt and pepper and add
to stock. Simmer ten minutes. Place mashed avocados in a
soup tureen, add cream and mix well. Add a few drops of

en coloring and stock. Stir and serve immediately with tortilla croutons which have been made by cutting tortillas into small squares and frying in three tablespoons shortening until golden brown. Bread cubes may be used instead. Yield: six servings.

SOPA DE PLATANO (*Banana Soup*)

10 red-skinned under-ripe bananas	1 teaspoon powdered cinnamon
¼ teaspoon cloves	Salt
¼ teaspoon orégano	4 tablespoons shortening

Cook whole bananas in one quart of water over low heat ten minutes. Remove bananas, peel and mash with cloves, orégano and cinnamon. Knead the mixture, add a pinch of salt and fry in shortening until browned slightly. Place on a serving dish and garnish with the following sauce:

Sauce

4 medium-sized tomatoes, drained and chopped	1 medium-sized onion, chopped
2 green peppers, peeled and chopped	¼ cup olive oil
	1 teaspoon salt

Fry tomatoes, peppers and onions about five minutes in olive oil and then add salt. Serve very hot. Yield: six servings.

SOPA DE FRIJOL NEGRO (*Black Bean Soup*)

1 pound small black beans	2 tablespoons lime juice
1 pound pork, cubed and fried	2 sprigs cilantro (or use parsley)
1 onion, chopped	8 radishes, chopped
2 teaspoons salt	

Soak beans in one quart of water overnight. Place over low heat and when boiling add pork and onion and season with salt. Simmer, covered, until tender enough to put through a sieve, about five hours. Add lime juice and garnish with cilantro or parsley and radishes. Yield: six servings.

CREMA DE ZANAHORIA (*Cream of Carrot Soup*)

6 *large carrots, pared*
1 *teaspoon sugar*
1 *teaspoon salt*
1 *quart milk*
2 *tablespoons butter*

2 *tablespoons flour*
¾ *cup cream*
1 *breast of chicken*
⅛ *teaspoon pepper*
Pinch of nutmeg

Cook carrots in enough water to cover with sugar and salt about fifteen minutes. Drain, grind, and mix with half the milk. Melt butter, add flour, brown and add rest of the milk. Simmer, stirring, about five minutes. Place cream and chicken breast in soup tureen. Add hot carrot and milk mixtures and season to taste with salt, pepper and nutmeg. Yield: six to eight servings.

SOPA DE ALMEJAS JAROCHA (*Jarocha Clam Soup*)

2 *garlic cloves*
4 *tablespoons olive oil*
3 *onions, chopped*
3 *medium-sized tomatoes, chopped*

1½ *dozen clams, boiled and shucked*
1 *teaspoon salt*
1 *teaspoon pepper*
1 *teaspoon paprika*

Brown garlic in hot oil, pressing with a fork to extract flavor. Add onions and brown lightly. Add tomatoes, which have been boiled and sieved, and fry together about five minutes. Turn into a kettle, add the clams, one quart of the clam broth, salt, pepper and paprika. Simmer covered one hour. Yield: six servings.

SOPA DE ALMEJAS (*Tuxpam Clam Soup*)

2 pounds clams in shells
1 small onion, chopped
½ cup butter
2 tablespoons flour

4 cups scalded milk
Salt, pepper and nutmeg to
    taste
1 egg white, stiffly beaten

Wash clams thoroughly, boil in half cup water until shells
open, remove from shells, keeping water in which they were
boiled. Chop half the clams with the onion and put in a
saucepan with clam broth. Simmer five minutes. Melt butter
in another saucepan and blend in flour. Add clams and
onion mixture, stirring constantly. Then add, while stirring,
milk, salt, pepper and nutmeg. Add whole clams and boil the
mixture slowly ten minutes. When ready to serve add and
stir in egg white. Yield: six servings.

SOPA DE PURE DE GARBANZOS (*Chick Pea Soup*)

1½ cups cooked or canned
    chick peas
1½ quarts stock
1 sausage, chopped and
    cooked
2 tablespoons shortening

2 cloves garlic, chopped
2 medium-sized onions,
    chopped
1 medium-sized tomato,
    chopped
Salt and pepper

Grind chick peas and cook in stock while preparing other
ingredients. Fry sausage in shortening about three minutes,
remove and fry garlic and onions in the same shortening for
two minutes. Add tomato and fry three minutes longer. Add
this mixture to the chick peas and stock. Strain. Add sausage,
season to taste and heat well before serving. Yield: eight to
ten servings.

SOPA DE GARBANZOS CAMPECHANA

(*Chick Pea Soup, Campeche-Style*)

1 large onion, chopped	*¼ teaspoon salt*
2 tablespoons shortening	*2½ cups stock*
1 cup canned chick peas	*1 tablespoon butter*
1 tablespoon flour	

Sauté onion in shortening until golden brown. Add chick peas, which have been drained, and fry two or three minutes. Then add liquid from peas and boil slowly five minutes. Add the flour which has been blended in two tablespoons of water, salt and stock, and simmer five minutes. Just before serving add butter. Yield: five servings.

SOPA MICHOACANA (*Sweet Corn Soup*)

12 ears of sweet corn	*½ teaspoon salt*
3 cups milk, scalded	*⅛ teaspoon pepper*
2 tablespoons butter	*3-ounce package cream*
1 large tomato, peeled and	*cheese, sliced*
chopped	
1 medium-sized onion,	
sliced	

Cut kernels from cobs and divide into halves. Mix half with milk. Fry other half in the butter, together with the tomato, onion, salt, pepper and cheese, about five minutes. Add to milk and corn mixture. Yield: six to eight servings.

SOPA DE PESCADO CAMPECUANA
(*Fish Soup, Campeche-Style*)

3 fish heads	¼ teaspoon pepper
4 cloves garlic	¼ teaspoon nutmeg
1 teaspoon marjoram	1 tablespoon shortening
2 sprigs mint	½ sweet pepper
3 sprigs corlander (optional)	4 medium-sized tomatoes,
2 green onion tops	chopped
1 medium-sized onion,	1 tablespoon lime juice
chopped	Salt
4 sprigs parsley, chopped	1 teaspoon flour
1 egg yolk	4 slices toast

Simmer seven minutes fish heads, three cups of water, two cloves garlic, marjoram, mint, cilantro and onion tops. Then remove fish from broth, shred edible meat and mix with one-half onion, two sprigs parsley, egg yolk, pepper and nutmeg. Shape mixture into small balls.

In another saucepan, heat shortening and fry other half of chopped onion, remaining garlic cloves, chopped, and sweet pepper. Add the rest of parsley and tomatoes. Add fish broth and balls, lime juice and salt to taste. Add flour blended with one-quarter cup water and simmer, stirring, ten minutes. Serve garnished with tiny squares of toast. Yield: six to eight servings.

SOPA DE LENTEJAS (*Lentil Soup*)

1 pound lentils	2 cloves garlic
1 medium-sized onion,	1 laurel leaf
chopped	Salt and pepper
5 thin slices bacon	

Soak lentils overnight in water to cover. Drain, measure liquid from beans and add enough water to make three quarts. Add onion, bacon, garlic, and laurel leaf. Cover, and simmer four hours. Season to taste with salt and pepper. Yield: six servings.

SOPA DE ALBÓNDIGAS (*Soup with Meat Balls*)

½ pound ground beef	*1 tablespoon flour*
½ cup of ground pork	*2 tablespoons shortening*
½ cup boiled rice, mashed	*1 small onion, chopped*
1 egg	*½ cup tomato pulp*
Salt and pepper to taste	*1 quart beef stock*

Mix meat with rice and egg. Season and shape into little balls the size of walnuts. Roll in flour and fry lightly in hot shortening. Remove and in the same pan brown onion and add tomato. Add beef stock and simmer five minutes. Add meat balls and simmer for one half hour or until thoroughly heated. Yield: six servings.

SOPA MEXICANA (*Mexican Soup*)

1 pound pork loin	*2 quarts stock*
2 tablespoons fat	*1 teaspoon salt*
1½ cups corn kernels	*½ teaspoon pepper*
2 cups zucchini, chopped	*1½ to 2 ounces cream*
4 large tomatoes, peeled	*cheese*
and chopped	*2 avocados, peeled and sliced*

Cut the pork into small portions and fry in fat fifteen to twenty minutes, pouring off fat as it accumulates. Five minutes before removing, add corn, zucchini and tomatoes. Heat stock, add meat and vegetables and simmer, covered, thirty minutes. Season to taste with salt and pepper. Before serving add cheese cut in small squares or thin slices and avocados. Yield: eight servings.

SOPA DE CAMARONES (*Shrimp Soup*)

4 tablespoons fat	1 teaspoon allspice
2 tomatoes, peeled, chopped and drained	2 teaspoons chopped parsley
2 large onions, chopped fine	1 cup stock (more for a thinner soup)
2 cloves garlic, chopped fine	1 teaspoon salt
¼ cup blanched almonds, chopped	2 pounds shrimp, cooked and chopped
¼ cup prunes, cooked, pitted and diced	1 cup scalded milk
¼ cup seedless raisins	3 slices bread, cut into tiny squares and fried

Heat fat in a skillet, add tomatoes, onions and garlic and fry five minutes over a low heat. Add almonds, prunes and raisins, and fry eight minutes. Add allspice and parsley and fry five minutes longer. Add stock and salt and simmer a few minutes, until all the ingredients are well seasoned. Then add the shrimp and simmer three or four minutes longer. Put some of this mixture in each soup plate and pour over it a little hot milk. Garnish with fried bread squares. Yield: six servings.

SOPA SENCILLA (*Simple Soup*)

1 pound beef with bone	1 large tomato, peeled, chopped and drained
1 clove garlic	
½ medium onion	1½ quarts water
⅛ teaspoon cumin	¼ cup rice, soaked and drained
½ teaspoon pepper	
2 teaspoons salt	4 avocados, sliced

Place all the ingredients except rice and avocados in a pot and simmer until the beef is tender or cook at fifteen pounds pressure about one hour. Drain and heat broth. Add rice, salt to taste and simmer till rice is tender, about one-half hour. Serve garnished with avocados. Yield: eight servings.

SOPA DE CALABACITAS (*Squash Soup*)

4 medium-sized zucchini	1 quart milk
3 tablespoons butter	Salt and pepper
1 onion, chopped very fine	½ cup cream
2 tablespoons flour	1 slice bread, cubed

Scrub zucchini and remove ends. Cook covered in a small amount of boiling, salted water until tender or about five minutes. Drain, reserving water, and chop thoroughly. Heat two tablespoons of butter in a pan and fry onion until yellow. Blend one cup of reserved water with flour until smooth and add to onion. Bring mixture to boil, stirring, add zucchini, milk, and salt and pepper to taste. Simmer ten minutes. Before serving add cream and bread which has been browned in butter. Yield: six servings.

SOPA TOLUQUEÑA DE CEBOLLA (*Toluca-Style Onion Soup*)

2 tablespoons butter	¼ cup Toluca or Gruyere
2 egg yolks, beaten	cheese, cubed
3 cups scalded milk	Salt and pepper
3 cups boiling meat stock	
1 cup onions, quartered and cooked	

Melt butter, blend in egg yolks. Add milk, stirring constantly. Add stock, onions, cheese, salt and pepper. Heat, stirring constantly and serve. Yield: 8 servings.

SOPA DE TORTUGA (*Sea Turtle Soup*)

1 pound fresh turtle meat, or eight-ounce can	½ tablespoon vinegar
3 cloves garlic	4 small green peppers, shredded
1 medium-sized onion, chopped	½ tablespoon marjoram
½ cup tomato purée	⅛ teaspoon salt
¼ cup claret or Burgundy wine	⅛ teaspoon pepper
⅓ cup olive oil	½ teaspoon ginger
	⅓ cup peas

Place canned or cooked meat in saucepan, cover with water and bring to a boil. (If fresh turtle meat is used, first cut it into small pieces, cover with two quarts of water and cook until tender. Pour off all but enough water to cover.) Add remaining ingredients and simmer slowly about fifteen minutes or until the vegetables are tender. Yield: six to eight servings.

SOPA DE TORTUGA, ESTILO CAMPECHE
(*Turtle Soup, Campeche-Style*)

2 medium-sized onions	½ teaspoon salt
3 medium-sized tomatoes, peeled	6-ounce can turtle meat, chopped
1 sweet pepper	10 olives, chopped
3 cloves garlic	1 teaspoon capers, chopped
2 tablespoons shortening	2 cups stock
1 clove	1 tablespoon vinegar
¼ teaspoon powdered cinnamon	2 tablespoons white wine
¼ teaspoon marjoram	1 teaspoon flour
⅛ teaspoon cumin	3 sprigs parsley, finely chopped
½ teaspoon pepper	3 slices toast

Chop onions, tomatoes, sweet pepper and garlic very fine and fry in shortening. Add spice, salt, turtle meat and broth, olives, capers, stock, vinegar and wine. Bring the mixture to a boil and add, while stirring, flour which has been blended with two tablespoons water. Add parsley. Boil five minutes and serve on small squares of toast. Yield: six servings.

SOPA DE NUEZ (*Walnut Soup*)

4 cups stock
⅓ cup chopped raw potato
½ cup finely chopped
   walnuts
½ cup light cream
Salt and pepper

Heat stock to the boiling point, add potato and boil twenty-five minutes. Add nuts and boil for another ten minutes. Remove from fire, add cream and salt and pepper to taste. Serve immediately. Yield: six servings.

MACARRÓN CON ESPINACAS
(*Elbow Macaroni and Spinach Soup*)

2 cups elbow macaroni
1 teaspoon minced onion
1 tablespoon fat
1 teaspoon minced garlic
½ cup tomato pulp
2 quarts stock
½ cup boiled chopped
   spinach
Salt and pepper
Grated cheese

Cook macaroni until almost tender in a large quantity of boiling salted water and drain. Fry onion in fat with garlic until lightly browned. Add tomato pulp and fry a few minutes longer. Add stock and boil five minutes. Add macaroni, spinach, salt and pepper to taste and cook ten minutes. Add cheese on serving. Yield: six to eight servings.

MACARRÓN CON CHILE (*Macaroni with Chili*)

2 cups boiled macaroni
1 onion, chopped
2 tablespoons fat
1½ teaspoons salt

1 red or green chili, peeled,
　seeded and chopped
2 cups tomato pulp
½ cup grated cheese

Cook macaroni and drain. Sauté onion in fat. Add salt, chili and tomato pulp and pour over macaroni. Place mixture in a buttered baking dish, cover with grated cheese and bake in a slow oven (325 degrees F.) until the cheese is brown or about twenty-five minutes. Yield: six servings.

TALLARINES MEXICANOS (*Mexican Noodle Soup*)

3 medium-sized tomatoes
1 onion, chopped
2 cloves garlic, chopped
2 tablespoons lard
½ cup chopped sausage

2 cups stock
Salt and pepper to taste
6 ounces noodles
¼ cup grated cheese

Broil tomatoes, peel, chop and drain. Add onion and garlic and fry in lard two or three minutes. Add sausage which has been peeled and cut into small pieces, and fry about fifteen minutes, or until the sausage is thoroughly cooked. Place mixture in a baking dish with stock, salt and pepper and heat slowly until it begins to boil. Add noodles and continue to cook until the liquid has evaporated. Sprinkle with grated cheese and broil until the top is a golden brown. Yield: six servings.

CORONA DE ARROZ (*Crown of Rice with Guacam*

1 cup rice	2 ounces Gruyere cheese, sliced
½ cup shortening	
1 medium-sized onion, chopped	2 ounces yellow American cheese, sliced
½ cup water	1 hard-cooked egg
2 cups milk	1 avocado
1 tablespoon salt	1 cooked carrot, sliced
6 tablespoons butter	1 small can peas
¼ cup bread crumbs	

Soak rice in hot water fifteen minutes, wash and drain. Heat shortening and fry rice with onion till mixture begins to brown, about 15 minutes. Pour off excess fat and add water. Simmer till water has been absorbed, add milk and salt. Cover, and simmer over a very low flame for about ten minutes or till almost dry. Add half of the butter in small chunks. Butter a ring mold and sprinkle with bread crumbs. Arrange layers of fried rice, slices of cheeses and little chunks of butter. Bake in a moderate oven (350 degrees F.) ten minutes. Turn out onto a serving plate and garnish with slices of hard-cooked eggs, strips of avocado, cooked carrots and peas. Fill center with guacamole sauce.

Guacamole Sauce

3 avocados	1 teaspoon salt
2 medium-sized tomatoes	½ teaspoon pepper
1 medium-sized onion, chopped	1 green pepper (or canned chili serrano), chopped
1 tablespoon cilantro (or use parsley)	

Mash the avocados with a wooden spoon, add peeled, chopped and drained tomatoes, onion and seasoning. Yield: six to eight servings.

SOPA TABASQUEÑA (*Tabasco-Style Soup*)

1 cup rice
¼ teaspoon saffron powder
1 egg
1 teaspoon salt
4 tablespoons shortening
2 cloves garlic, chopped
1 small onion, chopped
1 medium-sized tomato,
  chopped
1 sweet pepper, seeded,
  chopped

2 tablespoons seedless
  raisins
1 teaspoon capers
12 olives, chopped
1 sweet potato, cooked and
  chopped
2 medium-sized white po-
  tatoes, cooked, chopped
2 bananas, sliced
2 hard-cooked eggs,
  chopped
2 tablespoons butter

Cook rice, covered, in two cups of water and drain. Dissolve saffron in two tablespoons water, add the egg and a pinch of salt and stir into rice. Put a layer of half the rice in the bottom of a buttered baking dish. Then add a layer of the following ingredients which have been fried together in four tablespoons shortening for four or five minutes: garlic, onion, tomato, sweet pepper, raisins, capers, olives, sweet and white potatoes, banana, hard-cooked eggs and remaining salt. Cover with the remaining rice and dot with small chunks of butter. Bake in a hot oven (425 degrees F.) ten minutes. Yield: six servings.

ARROZ CON OSTIONES (*Oysters and Rice*)

½ pound rice, washed
1 cup lard
2 cloves garlic
1 large onion, chopped

¼ cup chopped parsley
2 dozen oysters
Salt
1 cup stock

Fry rice in lard till golden brown. Add garlic, onion and parsley. Drain off fat, add oyster liquid and a pinch of salt and simmer about fifteen minutes. When the liquid has almost evaporated, add stock and oysters and cook until the rice is almost completely dry. Yield: six servings.

ARROZ MEXICANO (*Mexican Rice*)

1 cup white rice	1½ tablespoons chopped
1½ cups hot water	onion
4 tablespoons shortening	2 teaspoons salt
½ teaspoon cumin seed	1 large tomato, chopped
¼ green pepper, chopped	2½ cups hot stock
1 clove garlic	

Soak rice in hot water twenty-five minutes, drain and let stand to dry for one hour. Heat shortening, add rice and fry till rice begins to brown. Add the cumin, pepper, garlic, onion, salt and tomato. When the liquid has evaporated, add stock, a little at a time, as needed, cover and cook over low heat until rice is soft and stock has been absorbed or about twenty-five minutes. Yield: six servings.

ARROZ SURIANO (*Rice, Southern-Style*)

1 cup rice	1¼ cups hot water
6 tablespoons butter	½ cup cream
2 tablespoons olive oil	½ cup shrimp
2 cloves garlic, minced	½ cup tuna fish
1 medium-sized onion,	1 cup ketchup
chopped fine	¼ teaspoon pepper
1 cup canned peas	2 pimientos, thinly sliced
1½ teaspoons salt	

Soak the rice in hot water until slightly swollen. Rinse well in cold water and drain. Fry in two tablespoons butter and the oil. Add garlic, onion, peas and one teaspoon salt, mix well and drain. Add half of the hot water and when it has been absorbed add the rest of the water and one-half of the cream. Cover and cook until rice is almost dry. Add shrimp and tuna fish. Grease a glass casserole or ring mold with two tablespoons of butter, fill with rice and press down. Stand it in an outer pan of hot water to keep hot while sauce is being made.

Heat remaining butter in a saucepan, add ketchup, remaining cream, salt and pepper and simmer a few minutes. Turn rice out on a platter and pour sauce over it, or in center of ring mold. Garnish with pimientos. Yield: six servings.

PAELLA A LA VALENCIANA (*Spanish Rice*)

½ pound rice	1 small can pimientos
½ cup olive oil	½ pound peas, shelled
1 tablespoon lard	½ broiler, cooked
2 large onions, chopped	½ pound cod or haddock,
2 cloves garlic, chopped	cooked
3 medium-sized tomatoes,	¼ pound shrimp
broiled, chopped and	½ pound shelled clams
drained	½ cup cooked or canned
2 cups stock	lobster meat
Salt, pepper and saffron to	
taste	

Pour boiling water over rice and let stand fifteen minutes. Drain and rinse several times in clear water. Heat olive oil and lard in a heavy pot or frying pan. Add rice and fry, stirring often, until golden in color. Add onions and garlic, brown and drain off excess fat. Add tomatoes and fry until liquid has evaporated. If necessary, pour mixture into a larger pot, add stock, salt, pepper, saffron, pimientos, peas, chicken and fish which have been cut into small pieces, shrimp, clams and lobster. Cook the mixture very slowly until rice is soft. Yield: six servings.

ARROZ TROPICAL (*Tropical Rice*)

½ pound rice, washed and soaked	½ cup butter
1 quart chicken stock	4-ounce package grated coconut
1 clove	

Boil together, covered, for ten minutes rice, chicken stock and clove. Add butter and coconut and cook until rice is well done. Yield: six servings.

SOPA DE FIDEO Y GARANZOS
(*Vermicelli and Chick Pea Soup*)

1 cup canned chick peas	2 tablespoons olive oil
1 onion, sliced	½ cup vermicelli
2 cloves garlic	⅛ teaspoon salt
1 large potato, diced	

Drain chick peas and mash. Add three cups hot water and boil five minutes. Add onion, garlic, potato, one tablespoon oil and boil ten minutes. Then add vermicelli, salt, other tablespoon of oil and cook until vermicelli is done. Yield: six servings.

SAUCES

Any discussion of Mexican sauces is complicated. There is not in this country, the arbitrary classification which exists in the United States and in many European countries. In Mexico, the sauce is most frequently an integral part of the dish.

Nogada, for example, a sauce made of finely chopped walnuts and spices, is not considered by itself. One has chilies or chicken or squash or other kinds of vegetables *en nogada*

—it is the special way of preparing the dish. You may hunt through a library of Mexican cookbooks, back even centuries through books beautifully written in flowing script and bound in vellum, without encountering nogada listed under sauces. Nogada, with its thick creamy subtlety and its gay décor of pomegranate seeds is not a thing apart.

There are, however, a few sauces which may be made separately and used with a variety of dishes. Most popular of these is guacamole, an elementary combination of avocado, onion, tomato and spices, which is a frequent accompaniment to Mexican meals. Guacamole is served with meat dishes, vegetables, Mexican rice and with sea food, and is an essential part of tacos, tortas and tostadas. Because of its piquant quality, it is good served with cocktails.

Two other popular sauces that are used much as catchup is in the United States—on a wide variety of dishes—are salsa cruda and salsa frita. The *cruda* is simply tomatoes, onion and chilies chopped fine and mixed with salt. *Frita* is the same thing but fried for varied flavor.

Sauces have been a part of the Mexican cooking tradition since time out of mind. The Aztecs called sauce *mole* (*molli*) and used a wide variety of sauces to accompany game and fish and fowl and were extraordinarily fond of them. The Spaniards, who had hopefully sent Columbus to seek out the land of spices, were impressed and enthusiastic about the possibility of further sauces with the wealth of seasonings and new ingredients he brought to hand.

It is highly appropriate that the elaborate mole with stewed turkey of the familiar legend, concocted by a Spanish nun in a Puebla convent, should have been nationalized, for it is the mestizo blend which *is* Mexico—Aztec richness of ingredients, Spanish artistry, an admixture of religion and conceived for a festive occasion. The product is as substantial and spicy as Mexico itself.

There are a few other sauces of separate distinction: pickled sauce for meat, parsley sauce, almond sauce, and of course, salsa borracha. This "drunken sauce" is the invariable accompaniment for barbacoa and quite frequently for roast meat at home.

Among regions which have special sauces, Campeche is

noteworthy, also Puebla and Yucatan, where ach
natto seed) gives a rich yellow color to the favo
which covers everything from tacos to pheasant.

Quite frequently, the sauce gives the dish its name: as
mole de olla, which is beef stewed with a rich sauce, and
Pipian de Pepita de Calabaza, which is meat fricasseed in
pumpkin seed sauce.

GUACAMOLE (*Avocado Sauce*)

3 large avocados, chopped
1 medium-sized onion,
    peeled, chopped
1 medium-sized tomato,
    peeled, chopped

2 small chilies, chopped
1 tablespoon olive oil
1 teaspoon vinegar
2 teaspoons salt

Mix all ingredients until creamy. If the sauce is made in
advance, be sure to store in a cool place with the avocado
seeds placed in the sauce to prevent its darkening. Serve on
lettuce leaves or in lettuce cups. Yield: about eight servings.

SALSA CAMPECHANA (*Campeche-Style Sauce*)

1 cup parsley, chopped very
    fine
6 cloves garlic, broiled and
    chopped fine
½ teaspoon pepper
2 tablespoons vinegar

1 large onion, chopped fine
½ cup olive oil
1 tablespoon butter
1 sweet pepper, seeded and
    chopped very fine

Allow parsley to stand in one-fourth cup water for two
hours, or until very soft and drain. Add garlic, pepper and
vinegar. Fry onion in hot olive oil until transparent. Add
parsley and simmer slowly for ten minutes. Add butter, re-

move from fire when melted and add sweet pepper. Serve with cooked fish or with cold meats. Yield: six servings.

SALSA BORRACHA (*Drunken Sauce*)

8 dried peppers
½ cup of pulque or dry white
   wine
1 clove garlic
16 small green tomatoes, or
   4 large red tomatoes

1 tablespoon olive oil
3 tablespoons grated cheese
1 onion, chopped
1 tablespoon orange juice,
   or
   ½ tablespoon lemon juice

Roast peppers lightly, peel and remove seeds. Dice and let stand in one-half cup of pulque or dry white wine. Grind garlic, tomatoes and peppers or mash to a pulp. Add pulque or wine, oil, cheese, onion and fruit juice. Yield: about twelve servings.

SALSA PARA PESCADO (*Sauce for Fish*)

2 large onions, chopped
3 tablespoons olive oil
2 large tomatoes, peeled,
   chopped and drained
2 green chilies, peeled,
   seeded and diced
¼ cup stock or hot water

3 sprigs parsley, chopped
¼ teaspoon orégano
1 teaspoon salt
½ teaspoon pepper
¼ teaspoon nutmeg
¼ cup sherry wine
15 olives, chopped

Fry onions until golden brown in olive oil. Add tomatoes and chilies and fry for three minutes longer. Add stock, parsley, orégano, salt, pepper and nutmeg and simmer ten minutes. Remove from fire. Add sherry and olives. Yield: eight servings.

SALSA SABROSA (*Savory Sauce for Fish or Vegetab.*)

1 egg yolk
¼ cup olive oil
1 teaspoon salt
½ teaspoon pepper
1 tablespoon vinegar
2 tablespoons tomato purée
or paste

1 tablespoon chopped
parsley
1 canned pimiento, finely
chopped

Beat the egg yolk thoroughly and add oil slowly as for mayonnaise. Add salt, pepper and vinegar and continue beating until stiff. Add the tomato purée, parsley and pimiento. Yield: six servings.

SALSA FRITA (*Fried Sauce*)

2 medium-sized tomatoes,
peeled
1 small onion
1 clove garlic

1 canned chili serrano
(Page 238)
1 teaspoon salt
2 tablespoons olive oil

Grind vegetables together, add salt and fry in olive oil over a low flame about five minutes. Serve hot. Yield: about eight servings.

SALSA PARA POLLOS FRITOS (*Sauce for Fried Chicken*)

1 pint stock
3 medium-sized tomatoes,
peeled, chopped
1 carrot, peeled and sliced
2 spring onions, chopped
2 cloves garlic
2 laurel leaves
¼ teaspoon thyme

¼ teaspoon marjoram
2 teaspoons chopped parsley
2 tablespoons olive oil
1 green pepper, chopped
fine
1 teaspoon salt
½ teaspoon pepper

Cook stock with tomatoes, carrot, onions, garlic and herbs thirty minutes and drain. Heat olive oil, add green pepper, cooked vegetables, salt and pepper and simmer for one minute. Yield: eight to ten servings.

SALSA DE PEREJIL Y ALMENDRAS (*Parsley Almond Sauce*)

1 cup chopped parsley, well packed
¼ cup almonds, blanched
3 tablespoons vinegar
6 tablespoons olive oil
1 teaspoon salt

Cook the parsley in one cup of water until tender and drain. Grind parsley with almonds and add vinegar, olive oil and salt. Yield: six servings.

SALSA ESCABECHE PARA CARNE (*Pickled Sauce for Meats*)

4 dried chilies
1 clove garlic
¼ teaspoon cumin
½ cup vinegar
1 teaspoon salt
1 laurel leaf
¼ teaspoon thyme
1 onion, chopped fine
1 cup zucchini, cooked and diced
½ cup peas, cooked or canned
½ pound potatoes, cooked, peeled and diced
2 tablespoons olive oil
½ package cream cheese

Remove seeds from chilies, and soak overnight. Drain and grind with garlic and cumin. Add vinegar, salt, laurel, thyme, onion, zucchini, peas and potatoes. Allow mixture to stand one day or longer. When the sauce is to be served with any meat, add the olive oil. Garnish with very thin slices of cream cheese. The sauce will keep if stored in a very cool place. Yield: eight to ten servings.

MOLE POBLANO (*Puebla Sauce*)

4 dried red peppers
4 dried black peppers
1 large tomato
1 onion
2 tablespoons sesame
1 cup shelled peanuts
4 tablespoons shortening

1 square (*ounce*) chocolate
¼ tortilla, fried
5 pimientos, chopped
2 cloves
1 small stick cinnamon
Pinch of aniseed

Roast peppers, soak and grind with tomato and onion. If a less "picante" variety of the traditional sauce is desired, first soak peppers in salted water for two or three hours. Fry the sesame and peanuts in shortening with chocolate, tortilla, pimientos and spices. When the chocolate has melted add peppers, one-quarter cup of water and salt to taste. Cook very slowly till thick. Yield: about three cups.

SALSA CRUDA (*Raw Sauce*)

2 medium-sized tomatoes,
  peeled
1 small onion
1 clove garlic
1 canned chili serrano
  (Page 238)

2 sprigs coriander (*or use
  parsley*)
1 teaspoon salt

Chop vegetables, add salt and mix well. This sauce is served especially with meats, Mexican rice and beans. Yield: about eight servings.

SALSA DE JITOMATE Y QUESO (*Tomato and Cheese Sauce*)

2 large tomatoes
4 small green chilies

2 tablespoons fat
3-ounce cream cheese, sliced

Heat tomatoes in water to cover and drain. Peel and grind with chilies. Add fat and cheese and the water in which the tomatoes were cooked. Simmer for three or four minutes. Yield: about six servings.

Chapter 3

Antojitos—Enchiladas, Sopes, Tacos, Tamales, Tostadas

THE MOST POPULAR STALLS in charity fairs, school festivals or "just outside the church" semireligious fiestas are those where antojitos are sold. And in every Mexican city, scores of small restaurants advertise antojitos as their only fare. Not unusually, some small unpretentious cafe becomes quite famous because its owner has a flair for mixing the piquant sauces or preparing the ingredients. Then people flock from miles around to eat the tacos made by Doña Maria or the crisp tostadas prepared by Carmelita.

Antojitos is the diminutive plural of antojo, which means a whim or capricious desire. Just how antojitos came to be so called is a mystery rooted in early colonial Mexico. They are part of everyday life and an important one of fiestas.

Practically every state of the Mexican Republic has its own particular antojitos. However two cities, Guadalajara and Puebla, boast the widest variety. Both cities are Spanish, yet antojitos are Indian, with corn prominent among the ingredients. Tamales, enchiladas, tacos, tostadas, chalupas and sopes are the most popular.

Tamales vary in size and ingredients from Mexico's northern border to the southern states of Chiapas and Tabasco and the peninsula of Yucatan, but all have corn as chief ingredient. The size of a cigar in the states of Tamaulipas and Nuevo León, the northern tamales have more "stuffing" than corn covering and are wrapped in dry corn leaves. In Veracruz, Oaxaca and all the southeast, tamales are wrapped in banana leaves and often flavored with mole sauces. In other sections of the country sweet tamales filled with raisins and candied fruit are more favored.

Enchiladas are tortillas wrapped around chicken, pork or cheese mixtures, and served with different sauces. Tacos are similar but usually toasted. Tostadas are made with fried

65

tortillas covered with shredded meat or beans, cheese, lettuce and sauce. Chalupas—the word means canoes—are made of the same corn meal or masa of the tortillas, but are about three times as thick and canoe-shaped. Sopes are round or oblong, much smaller than tortillas, and as thick as a chalupa.

Antojitos may be part of a meal or, more often, a snack to satisfy that particular desire for something special which the Mexican explains by saying, "se me antojó," meaning, "it became a sudden, capricious but overwhelming desire." These "desires," as far as antojitos are concerned, generally occur during the late afternoon or evening hours.

ENCHILADAS

3 medium-sized tomatoes, peeled
1 glove garlic
6 tablespoons shortening
1 teaspoon salt
12 tortillas

2 medium-sized onions, chopped
1 pound of meat or chicken, cooked and shredded
3 ounces grated cheese
12 radishes
Lettuce leaves

Chop tomatoes with garlic. Fry in one tablespoon of shortening until thickened. Add salt. Fry the tortillas in remaining shortening, turning to cook second side. In the center of each tortilla place one spoonful of tomato sauce, a bit of onion, a spoonful of the meat or chicken and sprinkle with cheese. Roll each tortilla to form a long cylinder, place in a serving dish, sprinkle with a little more cheese and garnish with radishes and lettuce leaves. Yield: six servings.

ENCHILADAS DE FRIJOLES (Enchiladas of Beans)

12 tortillas
1½ cups Mexican Fried Beans (Page 149)

¼ cup fat
1 teaspoon salt
1 cup cream

Spread the tortillas with beans, roll and pin with picks. Fry in fat to a golden brown. Place in a glass baking dish and bake in a moderate oven (350 degrees F.) five minutes. Just before removing from oven pour salted cream over them. Yield: six servings.

ENCHILADAS DE QUESO (*Cheese Enchiladas*)

12 tortillas
½ cup shortening
3 dried chilies
1 small onion, chopped
1 clove garlic, chopped
½ cup water

1 pound of pork, chopped
  and fried
2 ounces hard cheese,
  chopped
½ cup cream
1 tablespoon butter

Fry tortillas lightly in shortening. Soak chilies in cold water, drain, remove seeds and chop fine. Add onion, garlic and water. Cook the chili mixture in one tablespoon shortening until it thickens. Dip tortillas in this mixture and place in the center of each a spoonful of the pork and bits of cheese. Fold each tortilla and place a layer in a glass baking dish. Cover with another layer of tortillas. Pour cream over all and dot wth chunks of butter. Bake in a moderate oven (375 degrees F.) eight to ten minutes. Yield: six servings.

ENCHILADAS DE POLLO (*Chicken Enchiladas*)

2 cups cooked chicken,
  chopped
1 tablespoon raisins,
  scalded, chopped
1 tablespoon almonds,
  blanched, chopped
1 tablespoon chopped olives
12 tortillas
2 eggs, lightly beaten
1 cup lard

6 large tomatoes, peeled,
  mashed
1 onion, chopped
2 small green peppers,
  chopped
Salt and pepper to taste
1 onion, sliced
Radishes
Lettuce

Mix chicken, raisins, almonds and olives. Dip tortillas in egg and on each put some of the chicken mixture, roll and fasten with picks. Fry in hot lard. Fry tomatoes, onion, peppers, salt and pepper in the hot lard. Cover the tortillas with the sauce. Garnish with sliced onion, radishes and lettuce. Serve hot. Yield: six servings.

ENCHILADAS GUADALAJARA (*Enchiladas, Guadalajara-Style*)

2 *sweet peppers*	¼ *cup clotted cream*
2 *medium-sized tomatoes, peeled*	1 *teaspoon rum or brandy*
	Salt
1 *medium-sized onion*	12 *tortillas, fried*
4 *ounces shortening*	1 *small head lettuce*
2 *tablespoons milk*	*Radishes*

Remove seeds from sweet peppers and chop with tomatoes and onion. Fry in one tablespoon shortening about ten minutes. Add milk, clotted cream, rum or brandy and salt to taste. Cook about two minutes. Dip tortillas in sauce, place a tablespoon of the following filling on each and roll. Serve very hot, garnished with lettuce leaves and radishes. Yield: six servings.

Filling

2 *sweet peppers, chopped*	1 *large avocado, diced*
12 *ounces fresh cheese, mashed*	8 *radishes, chopped*

Mix peppers, cheese, avocado and radishes.

TAMALES DE ALMENDRA (*Almond Tamales*)

¾ *cup butter*	4 *cups nixtamalina flour*
1⅛ *cups sugar*	*(packaged or canned), or*
1¼ *cups almonds, blanched, ground*	4 *cups white corn meal*
	¾ *cup rice flour*
1 *cup milk*	1 *teaspoon baking powder*
	Leaves of corn

Cream butter until fluffy. Add sugar and almonds which have been mixed with the milk. Sift together flours and baking powder. Add to creamed mixture and blend well. Wash the corn leaves thoroughly and soak about two hours to soften. On each leaf spread a layer of the mixture. In the center, place a tablespoon of the following filling. Roll in tamale form, folding the ends over so that the filling will not drop out. Cook in pressure cooker at 15 lbs. pressure about one hour. Yield: one and one-half dozen tamales.

Filling

5 egg yolks, beaten	1 teaspoon vanilla
1 cup sugar	1 pint milk, scalded
2 tablespoons flour	

Mix all ingredients and cook over low heat, stirring constantly, about twenty-five minutes or until bottom of the pan can be seen. Remove from fire and cool before putting in tamales.

ENCHILADAS DE TASCO (*Enchiladas, Tasco-Style*)

2 cups sifted flour	3 eggs, separated
1 pinch salt	4 tablespoons fat
1 teaspoon baking powder	Butter
1 pint milk	

Sift together flour, salt and baking powder. Stir in the milk and strain. Beat the egg yolks to a pale lemon color and beat the whites stiffly. Blend flour mixture with yolks and fold in the egg whites.

Heat a little fat in a frying pan until very hot, and drop in a tablespoon of the batter, moving the pan around so that it spreads and covers bottom. When one side is golden, turn, and brown second side. Butter each crêpe as it is taken from the heat and pile together, covered with a napkin to keep warm.

Fill the crêpes with grated cheese or fried shredded pork meat prepared according to the recipe for Mochomos (page 121). Yield: one and one-half dozen.

TAMAL DE CAZUELA (*Tamale en Casserole*)

1 pound shortening	*2 tablespoons salt*
2 pounds nixtamalina	*1 cup stock*
(packaged or canned), or	*1 teaspoon baking powder*
2 pounds white corn	
meal	

Cream shortening, add nixtamalina or corn meal, salt, stock, and baking powder. Beat until a small ball of the batter will float in water. Grease a baking dish, seven or eight inches in diameter, and pour one-half the batter into it. Then add a layer of filling. Cover with remainder of batter and bake in a hot oven (425 degrees F.) until top is browned or about thirty minutes. Yield: eight servings.

Filling

3 dried chilies anchos	*4 cloves*
(Page 238)	*4 black peppers*
3 dried mulato peppers	*1 teaspoon powdered cinna-*
(Page 238)	*mon*
3 dried pasilla peppers	*1 square chocolate*
(Page 238)	*1 teaspoon salt*
½ cup fat	*1 teaspoon sugar*
2 canned tortillas	*1 cup stock*
2 ounces peanuts	*1 pound cooked pork loin,*
2 tablespoons sesame	*shredded*
4 medium-sized tomatoes,	*1 pound chopped beef*
peeled	*¼ cup vinegar*

Remove seeds from the three kinds of peppers. Fry in fat lightly with the tortillas, peanuts and sesame. When almost brown add the tomatoes which have been peeled and fry about three minutes longer. Remove and chop fried ingredients together with the cloves, peppers and cinnamon. Fry again a few minutes and add chocolate, salt, sugar, stock and pork. Cook over moderate heat for about ten minutes, or until the mixture is quite thick. Just before removing from fire, add vinegar.

TAMALES DE PICADILLO (*Chopped Meat Tamales*)

3 pounds pork
2 cups water
4½ tablespoons salt, approximately
2 cloves garlic
2 tablespoons chili powder
1 teaspoon pepper
2 cups shortening

¾ cup stock
2 pounds nixtamalina (packaged or canned), or 2 pounds white corn meal
1 tablespoon baking powder
100 corn leaves, approximately

Cook pork with water and two tablespoons salt, about twenty minutes. Drain and grind. Grind garlic with the chili powder, pepper and one teaspoon salt and fry in two tablespoons of fat. Add pork and fry five minutes. Add one-quarter cup of stock and continue to cook until the liquid has evaporated.

Cream the rest of the fat until it is fluffy, mix with the nixtamalina or corn meal to which the baking powder has been added. Beat for about five minutes. Add two tablespoons salt, cover and let the mixture stand for one hour.

Soak corn leaves in enough water to cover them for two or three hours, drain well. Spread a one-quarter-inch layer of the nixtamalina mixture on each leaf, place a tablespoon of the filling on top and fold leaf around. Cut off points of leaves.

Put enough corn leaves on the bottom of a pressure cooker to make a bed one-quarter-inch thick. Place enough tamales horizontally to fill bottom and continue to place them in orderly layers until all have been put in. Cover with a layer of corn leaves one-quarter-inch thick. Over that put a very damp napkin, tucking it in around the corn leaves and let stand covered about three minutes. Uncover, pour one cupful of warm water over the napkin and recover. Cook at 15 lbs. pressure for about one hour. Yield: about three dozen.

TACOS EXQUISITOS

6 tortillas	1 medium-sized onion,
3-ounce package cream cheese,	chopped
sliced	½ clove garlic, chopped
1 tablespoon all-purpose flour	½ teaspoon salt
1 egg	⅛ teaspoon pepper
⅔ cup shortening	1 cup stock
3 medium-sized tomatoes,	
peeled	

Cut the tortillas in halves and place a piece of cheese on each. Fold and fasten with picks. Sprinkle with flour and dip in beaten egg. Fry in shortening until golden brown. Place in another frying pan one tablespoon of shortening, the chopped tomato, onion, garlic, salt and pepper and fry five minutes. Add stock and cook until thickened. Dip the filled tortilla halves in sauce and fry very slowly another five minutes. Yield: six servings.

TACOS DE RAJAS (Tacos with Peppers)

2 medium-sized onions	½ cup clotted (sour) cream
½ cup shortening	2 ounces grated cheese
3 large sweet peppers	Salt to taste
3 large tomatoes	6 tortillas (bought)

Slice onions and fry in two tablespoons shortening. Peel peppers, seed and cut into strips. Add peppers and tomatoes to the fried onion and fry five minutes longer. Add clotted cream, cheese and salt and fry over very low heat two minutes. Put a tablespoon of the mixture in the center of each

tortilla, fold over and fasten with picks. Then fry the stuffed
tortillas in the remaining shortening and serve with the following sauce. Yield: six servings.

Sauce

1 medium-sized onion,
chopped
1 large tomato, peeled,
chopped, drained

⅛ teaspoon salt
⅛ teaspoon pepper
2 tablespoons shortening

Fry first four ingredients in shortening for five minutes.

TACOS POBLANOS (*Puebla-Style Tacos*)

6 Mexican sausages, chopped
1 cup fat
4 eggs, lightly beaten
12 tortillas
3 large tomatoes, peeled,
chopped and drained
1 large onion, peeled and
chopped

2 sweet peppers, peeled and
chopped
¼ cup water
3-ounce package cream
cheese, sliced
2 hard-cooked eggs, sliced

Fry the sausages in two tablespoons fat two minutes and
add eggs. On each tortilla, place a tablespoon of the mixture,
roll tortillas and pin each with a pick. Fry them lightly in
the remaining fat. Serve on a platter and cover with sauce.
To make sauce fry together tomatoes, onion and peppers five
minutes. Add water and simmer eight minutes. Pour hot
sauce over tacos. Garnish with cheese and hard-cooked eggs.
Yield: six servings.

TACOS DE SAN CRISTOBAL (*San Cristobal Tacos*)

1 cup sifted all-purpose flour
1 teaspoon sugar

3 eggs
1 tablespoon butter

Combine ingredients and beat until smooth. For each crêpe, which is to form a taco, five or six inches in diameter, pour about three tablespoons of the batter onto a hot greased griddle. When lightly browned, turn and brown the other side. Immediately place about two tablespoons of the following mixture on each and roll. Yield: six servings.

Filling

1 small onion, chopped fine	½ cup ham, cubed
1 clove garlic, chopped	1 teaspoon chopped parsley
1 tablespoon shortening	2 cups water
½ cup pork loin, cubed	Salt and pepper to taste
½ cup veal, cubed	1 tablespoon bread crumbs
½ cup chicken, white meat, cubed	12 almonds, chopped
	1 tablespoon raisins

Sauté onion and garlic in shortening till brown. Add meats and brown. Add parsley, water, salt and pepper, cover and cook over low heat three hours. Drain mixture from broth and shred or chop very fine. Return to stock, add bread crumbs, almonds and raisins and cook, uncovered, until liquid has evaporated.

TAQUITOS CON SALSA DE JITOMATE
(*Little Tacos with Tomato Sauce*)

1 pound pork loin, cooked	1 tablespoon raisins
4 tablespoons fat	2 tablespoons sherry wine
2 small onions, chopped	1 hard-cooked egg, mashed
1 sweet pepper, chopped	12 tortillas
6 tomatoes	Grated cheese
1 tablespoon capers	

Grind pork and fry in two tablespoons fat. When beginning to brown, add one onion, pepper and one tomato, peeled, drained and chopped. Simmer five minutes and add capers, raisins and sherry. Simmer three minutes over very low heat and add egg.

Cook the remaining tomatoes in three-fourths cup water with a teaspoon of salt. Drain and peel, reserving liquid. Fry second onion and the tomatoes in remaining two tablespoons fat. Add the tomato liquid and simmer five minutes. Moisten each tortilla well in the sauce. Place a tablespoon of the meat mixture on each tortilla, roll, fasten with picks and place in a greased glass baking dish. Pour the tomato sauce over them and if any meat mixture is left sprinkle on top. Sprinkle with grated cheese and bake in a moderate oven (350 degrees F.) five or six minutes or until thoroughly heated. Yield: six servings.

TORTILLAS DE HARINA (Flour Tortillas)

2 cups flour   1 tablespoon shortening
1 teaspoon salt   Cold water

Flour tortillas are used almost exclusively in the northern part of Mexico. Much larger in size, they make a neat envelope for a wide variety of fillings. Several commercial brands of masa harina are now on the market. However, you may make your own simply. Sift together flour and salt. Cut in the shortening and add enough cold water to make a stiff dough, about two-thirds of a cup. Knead on a lightly floured board, make small balls, roll as thin as possible and cook on a lightly greased griddle. Yield: eight to ten portions.

TORTILLAS DE HARINA FRONTERIZAS
(Flour Tortillas, Sweet or Salty)

2 cups flour   ½ cup shortening
1 teaspoon salt, or   ¼ cup water
  ¼ cup sugar

Sift flour with salt or sugar to make a mound on a pastry board. Make a depression in the center and put in fat. Mix until it achieves the consistency of corn meal. Add water, bit by bit, stirring and blending until dough can be rolled on the board without tearing. Form the dough into small balls and roll on a floured board into five- or six-inch pancakes, one-eighth inch in thickness. Place on a lightly greased griddle, not very hot, and cook about four minutes on each side. Yield: about twelve tortillas.

QUESADILLAS (*Cheese Tortillas*)

4 cups sifted flour	4 tablespoons butter
1 teaspoon baking powder	1 egg
3-ounce package cream cheese	

Sift flour with baking powder and mix with cheese which has been creamed thoroughly with a fork. Add butter and egg, mix well and allow mixture to stand fifteen minutes. Roll very thin on a floured board and cut into circles about five inches in diameter. On each "pancake" place a tablespoon of the following mixture, fold over and fry in deep hot fat (370 degrees F.). Yield: about two dozen.

Filling

1 cup cooked and boned chicken, chopped	⅛ teaspoon pepper
	⅛ teaspoon salt
1 small onion, chopped	2 tablespoons shortening
1 medium tomato, peeled, chopped	

Fry the chicken, onions, tomato, pepper and salt in shortening five minutes over a moderately hot flame.

TOSTADAS COMPUESTAS (*Garnished Toasted Tortillas*)

12 tortillas (*bought*)
¾ cup fat
½ cup Fried Beans (Page 149)
1 small head lettuce, chopped
1 cup boiled potatoes, diced
  and fried lightly
2 tablespoons vinegar
3 tablespoons olive oil
1 teaspoon salt

½ teaspoon pepper
2 chicken breasts, cooked
  and shredded
½ cup Guacamole
  (Page 59)
1 canned chilpotle,
  shredded (Page 238)
½ cup fresh soft cheese or
  cream cheese, mashed

Fry the tortillas in fat until well browned and drain. Fry
the beans, mashing them with a fork while they are cooking.
Spread a very thin layer of beans on each fried tortilla. Mix
lettuce, potatoes, vinegar, oil, salt and pepper and place a
layer on the beans. Cover with chicken, a tablespoon of
guacamole, a strip of chilpotle and a little mashed cheese.
Yield: six servings.

CHILAQUILES (*"Poor Man's Dish"*)

4 tortillas
Fat for deep frying
2 medium-sized tomatoes,
  peeled
2 green chilies (*or peppers*)
1 medium-sized onion

1 teaspoon salt
½ pound Monterey cream
  cheese or American
  cheese, sliced
¼ cup grated cheese

Cut tortillas in strips about one inch wide, and fry in deep
hot fat (360 degrees F.). Do not let them brown. Grind tomatoes, chilies and onion together, add salt and one-quarter
cup water. Mix thoroughly and fry in shallow fat about three
minutes. Add the cream cheese and cook three or four minutes longer over low heat until the cheese is soft. Add to

the fried tortillas and serve very hot, sprinkled with grated cheese. Yield: six servings.

HONGOS EN TORTILLAS (*Mushrooms in Tortillas*)

½ pound mushrooms
1 small onion, chopped
1 garlic clove, chopped
2 tablespoons fat
5 eggs, well beaten
1 teaspoon salt

½ teaspoon pepper
3 ounces cream cheese or light American cheese, sliced thin
6 tortillas (bought), fried

Wash the mushrooms well and chop. Fry with onion and garlic in fat fifteen minutes. Add the eggs, salt, pepper and cheese. Cook over low heat stirring constantly until the mixture has the consistency of thick cream. Serve on fried tortillas. Yield: six servings.

TOSTADITAS DE FRIJOL (*Bean Tostadas*)

6 tortillas
Fat
1 cup Bean Purée
½ small head lettuce
6 radishes, sliced
1 canned chilpotle, chopped (Page 238)

1 avocado, sliced
1 tablespoon grated cheese
1 Mexican sausage, cooked and chopped
1 teaspoon vinegar
1 teaspoon olive oil

Fry tortillas in fat until golden brown. In another frying pan heat bean purée and place a tablespoon on each tortilla, add a mound of chopped lettuce and garnish with radishes, chilpotle, avocado, cheese and sausage. Add a few drops of vinegar and a few drops of olive oil. Serve while still hot. Yield: six servings.

TOSTADITAS TAPATÍAS (*Tostadas, Guadajalara-Style*)

12 small thin tortillas   2 chilpotles, chopped
   (bought)   (Page 238)
Deep fat for frying   4 tablespoons grated cheese
4 Mexican sausages   Oil
¼ cup thick Bean Soup   Vinegar
½ head lettuce   Salt
1 avocado, chopped

Fry tortillas in deep hot fat (370 degrees F.) until golden brown. Drain. Fry separately until brown the sausage which has been cut into small pieces. Add bean soup and cook together over low heat five minutes. Spread tortillas with the mixture. Top with lettuce, chopped very fine, avocado and chilpotle and sprinkle with cheese. On serving, season with oil, vinegar and salt. Yield: six servings.

TOSTADAS SONORENSES (*Tostadas, Sonora-Style*)

6 tortillas   3-ounce package cream
1 cup fat   cheese
4 Mexican sausages   1 tablespoon olive oil
1 small head lettuce, shredded 1 teaspoon vinegar
·1 large onion, chop half and   1 teaspoon salt
   slice half   Tomato Cheese Sauce
                          (Page 63)

Fry tortillas one by one in fat until they are golden in color. Remove and drain on paper towelling. Fry the sausages in the same shortening. Drain and chop very fine. On each hot toasted tortilla place a bit of shredded lettuce, a tablespoon of the chopped sausage, a teaspoon of chopped onion and a tablespoon of cream cheese. Season with oil, vinegar and salt. Cover with Tomato Cheese Sauce and garnish with sliced onion. Yield: six servings.

SOPES JALISCIENSES (*Filled Corn Cakes, Jalisco-Style*)

1 pound nixtamalina
(packaged or canned), or
1 pound white corn meal
2 teaspoons salt
2 three-ounce packages
cream cheese, mashed
¾ cup fat
1 tablespoon chopped onion

1 clove garlic, chopped
1 large tomato, peeled,
chopped and drained
1 cup cooked beans, ground
½ teaspoon chili powder
1 small can sardines, drained
and boned

Mix nixtamalina or white corn meal with one teaspoon salt, cheese, one tablespoon fat and enough water to make a soft dough. Form pancakes about three and a half inches in diameter with a slightly raised border around the edge. Fry in fat to cover until golden brown. Fry onion and garlic in fat until golden, add tomato, beans, the remaining teaspoon salt and chili powder and fry five minutes. Remove from heat and mix with the sardines to form a paste. Fill the center of the cakes with the paste and heat in a moderate oven (375 degrees F.) a few minutes before serving. Yield: two dozen.

MOLOTES (*Stuffed Rolled Pancakes*)

1½ cups nixtamalina (packaged or canned), or
1½ cups white corn meal

1 tablespoon salt
½ pound cottage cheese
Fat for deep frying

Mix enough water with the nixtamalina or corn meal to form a dough. Add salt and cottage cheese. Mix well, pat into thin pancakes and roll around a thin round wooden spoon handle so that they resemble enchiladas. Fry until golden brown in deep hot fat (350 degrees F.) and fill with the following mixture:

Filling

1 *pound Monterrey cream cheese or white American cheese, chopped*	1 *cup canned salmon*
	1 *teaspoon salt*
	½ *teaspoon pepper*
1 *canned chili Jalapeño, shredded* (Page 238)	

Mix ingredients thoroughly before stuffing the pancakes. Heat five to ten minutes in a very slow oven (275 degrees F.). Cover with Salsa Frita (Page 61). Yield: one and one-half dozen.

BURRITOS (*Little Burros*)

2 *cups nixtamalina (packaged or canned), or* 2 *cups white corn meal*	1 *teaspoon salt*
	Warm water
	Chicharrones (Page 206)

Mix nixtamalina or white corn meal and salt. Add enough water to make a stiff dough and set aside for twenty minutes. Wet hands in water and mold balls of dough the size of a walnut. Pat into one-quarter-inch cakes. Make a depression in the center of each and fill with chicharrones. Bake in a moderate oven (350 degrees F.) ten to fifteen minutes. Yield: three dozen. (Burritos in the northern part of Mexico and in the southwestern part of the United States are quite different. Now a popular dish in many restaurants and taco stands in California and Texas are northern burritos, which are made by folding a flour tortilla around a mound of re-fried beans, seasoned to taste with chili.)

EMPANADAS DE VIGILIA (*Turnovers*)

½ cup butter   2 egg yolks
½ cup shortening   1 teaspoon salt
4 cups flour

Mix the first three ingredients gently with the fingers.
Make a mound on a pastry board with a center depression
and in the depression put the egg yolks, half teaspoon salt
and one-quarter cup cold water in which the other half teaspoon of salt has been dissolved. Mix well, form into small
balls and flatten into tortilla-shaped rounds about one-eighth
inch thick and five inches in diameter. Place one and a half
tablespoons of one of the following fillings on each, and fold
dough over, pasting edges together with lightly beaten egg.
Place on greased baking sheet, let stand ten minutes and bake
in a moderate oven (375 degrees F.) ten minutes. Serve with
olive sauce. Yield: about eighteen.

Filling I

1 pound red snapper, cooked,   1 cup olive oil
   boned and shredded   3 hard-cooked eggs, chopped
1 cup cream   1 slightly beaten egg

Mix all ingredients.

Filling II

2 dozen oysters, drained,   2 hard-cooked eggs, chopped
   chopped   2 tablespoons finely chopped
1⅓ cups cream   parsley

Mix the ingredients.

Filling III

2 fresh, peeled tomatoes	2 teaspoons grated cheese
1 large onion, chopped fine	Orégano (pinch)
2 cans boneless sardines	Salt and pepper
2 hard-cooked eggs, chopped	

Mix the ingredients thoroughly.

Filling IV

1 pound dry codfish   ½ cup olive oil

Put the codfish which has been soaked for twenty-four hours in a pot with cold water and cook three hours. Remove bones, shred finely and fry in the oil three or four minutes over moderate heat.

Olive Sauce

2 large onions, chopped	4 tomatoes, peeled and
3 cloves garlic, chopped	chopped
½ cup olive oil	Salt and pepper to taste
2 canned pimientos, chopped	20 pitted olives, chopped

Fry onions and garlic in oil until slightly brown, add pimientos, tomatoes, salt and pepper and fry eight to ten minutes. Remove from fire and add olives.

Chapter 4

Sea Food

WHEN BERNAL DIAZ Del Castillo, an old man and in his eighty-fourth year, sat down to write the history of the New World he had helped to conquer with Cortes and the other four hundred and more who had disembarked at Veracruz, he remembered "as though it were yesterday" the way the Aztec capital had been. He remembered the towering pyramids and the palaces of Tenochtitlan gleaming in the sun. He remembered the tortuous climb, the ambuscades, the weariness. He remembered the honors which had been given to the miraculous strangers on horseback—the jewels, the cloaks, the bars of gold and silver and the wonderful food.

One of the dishes which most pleased the Spaniards had been the sea food, relayed by more than three hundred runners from the port city to the high plateau to the palace of Moctezuma, last of the New World imperial gourmets.

Then as now fish for the Mexicans did not mean fasting. And the Alvarados, the Diazes and others who found it a royal treat centuries ago, added to it the subtle ways of preparation and the savory sauces which they had known back in the Old World. Some of the sea-food dishes were only slightly influenced. Others, like the people of Mexico, became a mestizo blend of Indian art and sophisticated Spanish artistry. Still others remain pure Spanish in origin— like paella.

A traditional Spanish dish, paella has been incorporated into the Mexican diet and is so universally popular it is considered a national dish. Comprised of a variety of fish and other sea foods, it is never ready-made except on the special weekly "paella days" which many restaurants advertise. Ordering it always involves an hour's wait for talk or a game of dominoes.

In addition to the eclectic school of cookery, there is also an original tradition which flourishes throughout the country.

Every state and region has its specialty, the secrets of which are carefully guarded for fiesta time. The specialty of Campeche on the Gulf Coast is the gigantic shrimp. In Baja California, it is the wonderful sea turtle from which richly flavored soups are made, steaks are cut and the shells proudly mounted for ornaments. Fish in the beautiful west coast resort of Acapulco means seviche, the raw pieces of meat cut up, pickled and served with stinging sauce, or the tiny live clams that are served in their shells.

Sea food is important in the diet of the people of the Isthmus of Tehuantepec, and a gourmet's treat beyond belief, is a picnic beneath the pepper and palm trees with shrimp roasted on the embers of a great bonfire and quantities of chilled coconut milk.

But, most of all, sea food is associated with Veracruz.

Every fish lover in Mexico makes regular pilgrimages to this most historic port city which has been the scene of all invading attempts from Cortes to General Scott and Maximilian. Veracruz is the city of gaiety in Mexico. From the palm-lined shores of the Mocambo beach to the center where curious little Toonerville trolleys ply back and forth, there is music and dancing and eating with rare gusto.

These things are always part of Veracruz even after the town has settled into the Lenten afterglow of the Mardi Gras season. There is always good eating. The memory of Veracruz is the memory of hot tropical days and warm tropical nights with the wind crackling the palm leaves. It is the lazy luxury of sitting in the portales around the plaza watching the boys and girls of the city promenade in the paseo around and around the plaza fountain while waiters carry foaming tarros of Orizaba beer to the bare board tables and bring huge plates of shrimp, spicy and savory, or smoking stuffed crabs to the late evening diners.

BACALAO (*Codfish*)

1 pound onions, peeled and
  sliced
3 cloves garlic, chopped
1½ pounds dried codfish *
1 pound tomatoes, peeled,
  chopped, drained
1 teaspoon salt
2 small green chilies,
  chopped
½ cup olive oil

Place a layer of onions and garlic in a casserole. Over it, spread a layer of codfish which has been cut into tiny pieces. Repeat layers until the three ingredients have been used. Cover with a sauce made by mixing the tomatoes with the salt and chilies. Pour the olive oil over all. Bake in a slow oven (300 degrees F.) thirty to forty minutes or until the sauce has thickened. Yield: six servings.

PESCADO EXQUISITO (*Exquisite Fish*)

3- to 5-pound fish (mackerel,
  bluefish, cod, haddock)
Juice of two limes
2 tablespoons salt
Juice of two sour oranges
½ teaspoon chili powder
1 tablespoon butter
1 cup peeled cooked shrimp
¼ cup vinegar
1 teaspoon pepper
2 cloves garlic, broiled and
  mashed
1 sweet pepper, seeded and
  chopped fine
1 small onion, chopped fine
3 medium-sized tomatoes,
  peeled, chopped and
  drained
Olive oil

Clean fish and cut lengthwise, but without separating the two halves. Soak in enough water to cover with the lime juice and one teaspoon salt for ten minutes. Remove and dry. Cover inside with orange juice which has been mixed with chili powder and one teaspoon salt. Then butter the inside. Soak shrimp for one hour in the vinegar mixed with one tea-

* If cod is too strong, soak in cold water one hour.

spoon of salt, pepper, garlic, sweet pepper, onion and tomatoes. Drain shrimps and use to stuff fish. Pour a little olive oil over the incision and tie to close. This is done in Mexico with strips of banana leaf but cord may be used in the United States. Butter a banana leaf or parchment cooking paper and cover the bottom of a glass baking dish. Put the fish on leaf or paper and cover with another leaf or piece of heavy greased paper. Bake in a moderate oven (375 degrees F.) thirty-five to forty minutes or until easily flaked and moist. Yield: six servings.

PESCADO EN SALSA DE ALMENDRAS (Fish in Almond Sauce)

2 pounds red snapper, sliced
1 tablespoon salt
1 teaspoon pepper
6 tablespoons olive oil
1 cup blanched almonds, chopped fine or ground

3 hard-cooked eggs
3 tablespoons French mustard
1 tablespoon chopped parsley
2 lemons, sliced

Wash fish, dry and place in a glass baking dish; sprinkle with half the salt and pepper and pour three tablespoons of olive oil over them. Bake in a moderate oven (350 degrees F.) fifteen minutes. Mix almonds, mashed egg yolks, mustard, three tablespoons of olive oil, parsley and chopped egg whites, and the remaining salt and pepper. When fish is done, bathe with this sauce and garnish with lemon slices. Yield: six servings.

PESCADO EN SALSA DE AJO (Fish in Garlic Sauce)

2 pounds red snapper or sea bass fillets, or any similar fresh or frozen fish
6 cloves garlic, minced
6 tablespoons olive oil

2 oranges
1 teaspoon pepper
2 tablespoons chopped parsley
1 teaspoon salt

Arrange fillets side by side in a greased baking dish. Mix three cloves garlic with three tablespoons olive oil and spread mixture over fillets. Squeeze the juice of one orange over all and sprinkle with pepper. Bake in a hot oven (450 degrees F.) about twenty minutes or until the fish is easily flaked. Fry the rest of the garlic in remaining olive oil. Remove garlic and fry parsley three minutes. Add the juice of the other orange, salt and a little pepper. Pour sauce over the fish before serving. Yield: six servings.

PESCADO EN VERDE (*Fish in Green Sauce*)

2 pounds fresh or frozen fish fillets
Juice of one lime
3 teaspoons salt
1 sprig parsley, chopped fine
1 large onion, chopped fine
2 sweet peppers, chopped fine
1 cup cooked peas

3 cloves garlic, broiled and chopped
4 green tomatoes, peeled and chopped
½ teaspoon pepper
1 tablespoon vinegar
2 tablespoons olive oil

Wash fish and soak in enough water to cover with lime juice and one teaspoon of salt. Mix parsley, onion, sweet peppers, peas, garlic, tomatoes, pepper, one teaspoon salt and the vinegar. Stir well and dip fish in sauce. Place the fish in a greased pan or baking dish and cover with the remaining sauce. Cover and simmer over low heat ten to fifteen minutes or until the sauce is almost dry. Add the olive oil and simmer another three or four minutes. Yield: six servings.

PESCADO FRÍO CON GUACAMOLE
(*Chilled Fish with Gaucamole*)

2 pounds fresh or frozen fish fillets
3 tablespoons lemon juice
1 pound small onions, peeled
1 teaspoon salt
½ teaspoon thyme
½ teaspoon laurel
½ teaspoon marjoram

2 tablespoons olive oil
1 tablespoon vinegar
½ teaspoon pepper
1¼ cups Guacamole (Page 59)
1 canned chili in vinegar, cut into strips
15 olives

Bake the fish in a hot oven (400 degrees F.) with lemon juice, onions, salt, thyme, laurel and marjoram till it flakes easily. Place fish on serving dish with onions, pour olive oil and vinegar mixed with pepper over the fish and chill. Cover with Guacamole and garnish with chili and olives. Yield: six servings.

PESCADO EN AVELLANA (*Fish in Hazelnut Sauce*)

2 pounds haddock, cod or mackerel	½ cup milk
	1 cup grated cheese
Salt and pepper	¼ cup cooking sherry
2 tablespoons lemon juice	1 pinch nutmeg
6 tablespoons butter	½ cup bread crumbs
1 pound hazel nuts, ground	

Cut fish in slices and remove bones. Mix salt and pepper with lemon juice, brush fish slices and let stand one hour. Place in a greased baking dish and rub well with butter. Mix the nuts, milk, grated cheese and sherry. Pour sauce over fish slices, covering them completely. Sprinkle with a little salt, pepper and nutmeg and add bread crumbs. Dot with chunks of remaining butter. Bake in a very hot oven (450 degrees F.) about thirty minutes. Yield: six servings.

PESCADO EN SALSA DE MOSTAZA (*Fish in Mustard Sauce*)

3- to 5-pound fish, as mackerel	½ cup olive oil
	1 teaspoon pepper
1 teaspoon salt	3 tablespoons butter
2 tablespoons lemon juice	1 tablespoon powdered mustard
2 cloves garlic, broiled	
1 tablespoon parsley	1 teaspoon flour

Soak fish in enough water to cover with the salt and lemon juice for fifteen minutes. Drain and dry. Chop the garlic with the parsley and add oil and pepper. Cover fish well with this sauce and allow to stand for ten minutes, turning fish twice. Grease a piece of heavy paper, put it in a pan and place the pan over very low heat. Put fish on the paper and cook slowly, pouring a tablespoon of oil mixture over it from time to time till fish is tender. Heat butter and add mustard and flour, stirring well. Remove from fire after two or three minutes and add this to the remaining parsley-oil mixture by teaspoonfuls. Cover fish with this before serving. Yield: six servings.

PESCADO EN PEREJIL (*Fish in Parsley*)

2 pounds fish fillets, any
   variety
2 tablespoons lemon juice
2 teaspoons salt
½ cup olive oil
1 cup ground parsley

2 thin slices bread
2 cloves garlic, chopped
½ teaspoon pepper
¼ teaspoon cumin
2 tablespoons vinegar

Soak fillets in half the lemon juice and one teaspoon salt in sufficient water to cover. Transfer to another pan, add enough water to cover and the other teaspoon salt and cook five minutes. Heat four tablespoons olive oil in a saucepan, add parsley and bread, which has been soaked in water and crumbled in small pieces, garlic, pepper and cumin and fry five minutes. Add this to the fish with its broth and simmer another five minutes. Remove from heat and add vinegar and remaining oil. Yield: six servings.

PESCADO EN SALSA BLANCA (*Fish in White Sauce*)

2 lemons
2 pounds fish, as mackerel
¼ teaspoon laurel
¼ teaspoon orégano
¼ teaspoon marjoram
1 stick cinnamon
1 teaspoon pepper
8 black peppercorns
3 teaspoons salt
3 cloves garlic
1 teaspoon parsley

2 tablespoons olive oil
2 onions, chopped fine
15 olives
2 tablespoons flour
1 cup milk
1 tablespoon butter
½ teaspoon nutmeg
1 teaspoon French mustard
3 eggs hard-cooked, sliced
2 pimientos, cut into strips

Cut two slices of lemon, reserve, and moisten fish with juice of remaining lemons. Simmer fish for ten minutes with one cup water, the two slices of lemon, laurel, orégano, marjoram, cinnamon, pepper, peppercorns, two teaspoons salt and garlic. Remove fish from liquid and place in a buttered glass baking dish. Bake in hot oven (425 degrees F.) fifteen minutes.

Fry the parsley in the olive oil with onions and olives and then pour on top of the fish. Blend flour with milk; add butter, nutmeg and one teaspoon of salt and boil, stirring, till thickened. Remove from fire, add mustard and pour over the fish. Garnish with eggs and pimientos. Yield: six servings.

PAN DE CAZON (*Fish Loaf*)

1 pound whitefish or butterfish	1 cup black beans, cooked
4 medium-sized onions, chopped	3 large tomatoes, peeled and chopped
1 tablespoon salt	1 canned chili serrano
1¼ cups fat	(Page 238)
1½ teaspoon epazote (or use dried parsley)	12 tortillas

Simmer fish in a very small amount of water with one onion and one teaspoon salt about fifteen minutes. Remove fish meat and mash with a fork. Fry fish meat slowly in one-quarter cup of fat with one onion and one teaspoon epazote (or parsley) until dry but not brown, about ten minutes.

Prepare Frijol Colado y Chile Frito (below).

Frijol Colado (*Bean Purée*)

Drain beans and grind. Fry in one-quarter cup fat with one teaspoon salt, one-quarter teaspoon epazote (or parsley), one onion and about one-half cup bean broth until mixture has the consistency of a purée. Reserve.

Chile Frito (Fried Chili)

Fry tomatoes, one onion, one-quarter teaspoon epazote (or parsley) and one teaspoon salt in one-quarter cup fat about five minutes. Before sauce dries, add chili serrano and three-quarters cup water. Simmer about five minutes but not until thickened.

Dip tortillas in Chile Frito (above) and fry in remaining fat without toasting. Place separately in a baking dish. Top each with a thick layer of Bean Purée and then with the fish meat. Cover with another tortilla and put a tablespoon of Chile Frito on each. Bake in a moderate oven (350 degrees F.) five minutes. Serve very hot. Yield: six servings.

TIQUINPAAT (Fillets with Guacamole Sauce)

2 pounds fish fillets, fresh or frozen
2 canned chilies serranos (Page 238)
⅛ teaspoon epazote (or use dried parsley)
1 teaspoon salt
12 tortillas (bought)
Guacamole (Page 59)

Broil fillets under medium heat for ten to twelve minutes. Remove. Grind together with the chilies. Add the epazote or parsley and the salt. Serve with hot tortillas and guacamole. Yield: six servings.

FILETES DE PESCADO A LA TAPATÍA (Fish Fillets, Jalisco-Style)

6 fillets of red snapper one-fourth inch thick
1 teaspoon salt
2 tablespoons lemon juice
½ teaspoon pepper
1 pimiento, cut in six slices
6 slices bacon, cut in halves lengthwise

Soak fillets in enough water to cover with a little salt and lemon juice for ten minutes. Remove and drain. Sprinkle each fillet with pepper and salt, spread a slice of pimiento on each and roll. Wrap each end with a piece of bacon and fasten with picks. Place the rolled fillets on a glass baking dish and bake in a hot oven (425 degrees F.) for ten to fifteen minutes. Yield: six servings.

PESCADO DEL CARMEN (*Fish, Carmen-Style*)

2 pounds fish slices
2 tablespoons lemon juice
1 teaspoon salt
6 tomatoes, peeled, chopped and drained
2 onions, chopped fine

1 sweet pepper, seeded and chopped
1 tablespoon vinegar
½ teaspoon pepper
2 tablespoons olive oil
1 clove garlic
1 tablespoon butter

Wash the fish slices and soak ten minutes in enough water to cover with lemon juice and salt. Drain and rinse twice. Mix tomatoes, onions, sweet pepper, vinegar and pepper. Heat olive oil in a saucepan or deep frying pan and cook a clove of garlic in it about three minutes. Remove. Fry the tomato mixture in the olive oil for about five minnutes. Dip the fish portions in this sauce and place them in a buttered casserole or glass baking dish. Pour the remaining sauce over them. Cover and cook over low heat fifteen minutes. Remove cover and let simmer five minutes longer. Add dots of butter and serve hot. Yield: six servings.

PESCADO MAZATLECO (*Fish, Mazatlan-Style*)

1 quart water
1 pound fresh robalo (haddock) or huachinango (red snapper)
½ lemon
1 laurel leaf
¼ teaspoon salt
Tops of two young onions, chopped
4 whole black peppers

2 cloves
1 medium-sized onion
1 clove garlic
3 tablespoons olive oil
3 medium-sized tomatoes
1 teaspoon parsley, chopped fine
1 small pickled pepper, chopped
1 tablespoon bread crumbs

Simmer together, covered, for ten minutes water, fish, lemon, laurel leaf, salt, onion tops, black peppers and cloves. Remove from fire. Fry onion and garlic in oil until onion is lightly browned. Add tomatoes which have been peeled, chopped and drained and the parsley and fry for three or four minutes over low flame. Add two tablespoons of the fish broth to the fried mixture. Remove the pan from the heat and add the fish, shredded, and the pickled pepper. Mix ingredients together and place in a greased glass baking dish. Sprinkle with bread crumbs and bake in a hot oven (425 degrees F.) ten or fifteen minutes. Serve very hot. Yield: three servings.

PESCADO VERACRUZ (Fish, Veracruz-Style)

½ cup olive oil	½ teaspoon sugar
1 tablespoon chopped onion	½ teaspoon lemon juice
1 clove garlic, minced	6 fish fillets or slices
2 cups tomato sauce	(haddock or cod)
2 tablespoons red chili powder	3 potatoes, boiled
2 ground peppercorns	18 pitted olives
⅛ teaspoon cinnamon	3 slices bread, cut in triangles
2 ground cloves	2 tablespoons butter

Heat half the olive oil and fry onion and garlic until transparent. Add tomato sauce and spices and fry about five minutes. Add sugar and lemon juice and a little water if the sauce seems too thick. Heat remaining oil and fry fish. Add to the sauce. Add potatoes, cubed, and simmer three minutes over low heat. Garnish with olives and bread which has been fried in butter. Yield: six servings.

ROBALO EN PEREJIL (Haddock in Parsley Sauce)

3 large tomatoes	6 half-inch slices haddock or
2 large onions	cod or, preferably, red
1 sprig parsley	snapper
2 whole black peppers	½ cup olive oil
1 clove	Salt and pepper
2 cloves garlic	2 small chilies
¼ cup vinegar	18 stuffed olives

Chop tomatoes, onions and parsley. Grind black peppers, clove and garlic and mix with the vinegar. Place a layer of the tomato mixture in a greased casserole, then a layer of fish slices, then some of the vinegar mixture and a tablespoon of oil. Season with salt and pepper. Repeat layers until ingredients have been used. Garnish with chilies and olives. Bake in a hot oven (400 degrees F.) thirty minutes. Yield: six servings.

PÁMPANO CAMPECHANO (*Pompano, Campeche-Style*)

2 pounds pompano	½ teaspoon orégano
6 tablespoons lemon juice	4 cloves garlic, chopped
1 teaspoon salt	6 cumins
2 tablespoons olive oil	1 onion, sliced
1 teaspoon chili powder	1 tablespoon fat, melted
½ teaspoon pepper	

Soak the fish in lemon juice with salt for half an hour. Remove fish and rub inside and out first with olive oil and then with mixture of spices. Place in a greased casserole, cover with onion slices and brush with fat. Bake in a moderate oven (350 degrees F.) twenty-five to thirty minutes. Drain off liquid, keep it hot and broil fish three or four minutes. Before serving, pour reserved liquid over fish. Yield: six servings.

HUACHINANGO MARIA TERESA (*Red Snapper, Maria Theresa*)

2 pounds red snapper	4 tablespoons cream
Salt and pepper	1 tablespoon butter
2 teaspoons chopped parsley	4 tablespoons bread crumbs
4 eggs slightly beaten	1 canned chili, sliced
2 red peppers, chopped	

Boil the fish in enough salted water to cover, with pepper to taste, and parsley about fifteen minutes or until tender. Remove, drain and separate fish from bones. Shred the fish and mix with eggs. Add the chopped peppers and the cream. Butter a casserole and sprinkle with bread crumbs. Put in the fish mixture, pressing it down well. Bake in a slow oven (325 degrees F.) fifteen or twenty minutes. Garnish with chili. Yield: six servings.

HUACHINANGO EN TOSTADAS (*Tostadas with Red Snapper*)

1 pound red snapper	1 small onion, chopped fine
1 teaspoon salt	3 tomatoes, peeled,
1 teaspoon laurel	chopped and drained
1 teaspoon thyme	3 sprigs parsley, chopped
1 teaspoon marjoram	fine
½ teaspoon pepper	10 olives, chopped
1 clove garlic	12 tortillas
1 tablespoon vinegar	¼ cup fat
2 tablespoons olive oil	Shredded lettuce

Cook fish in one cup water with the salt, laurel, thyme, marjoram, pepper, garlic and vinegar fifteen minutes or until fish can be flaked with a fork. Drain and shred. Fry in the olive oil for five minutes onion, tomatoes and parsley and then add the shredded fish and the olives. Fry tortillas in fat until lightly toasted. Spread on each a spoonful of the fish, a layer of shredded lettuce and sprinkle with the hot fat in which the tortillas were fried. Yield: six servings.

MOJARRAS EMPANIZADAS (*Breaded Mojarras*)

6 mojarras (or use any small fish)	3 cloves garlic
	6 sprigs parsley
¼ teaspoon pepper	2 avocados, sliced
2 teaspoons salt	1 large green sweet pepper,
2 lemons	shredded
2 eggs, beaten lightly	1 tablespoon diced chili
2 cups bread crumbs	Jalapeño (Page 238)
2 cups olive oil	

Clean fish and make lengthwise incisions on both sides. Mix pepper and salt with juice of one lemon and rub fish well. Allow fish to stand in the refrigerator one hour. Remove and dip in the eggs, then in the bread crumbs, making sure that fish are well covered on both sides. Heat oil and brown the peeled garlic. Remove garlic and fry the fish one at a time to a golden brown. Drain on paper towelling. Garnish with parsley, the other lemon sliced, avocados and sweet pepper and season with chilies. Yield: six servings.

LANGOSTINOS CON RAJAS (*Crayfish with Pepper Strips*)

3 medium-sized green or red peppers, peeled and shredded

1 medium-sized onion, sliced thin

1 clove garlic, chopped

1½ tablespoons fat

3 medium-sized tomatoes, peeled, mashed

3 dozen cleaned and cooked crayfish or shrimps

1 teaspoon salt

¼ teaspoon pepper

Sauté peppers, onions and garlic in fat until browned. Add tomatoes and fry two or three minutes over medium heat. Add crayfish, salt and pepper and fry for about eight minutes longer over very low heat. This dish is often served with rice. Yield: six servings.

JAIBAS RELLENAS (*Stuffed Crabs, Veracruz-Style*)

12 crabs

2 sprigs parsley, chopped

¼ cup almonds, blanched and ground

2 tablespoons seedless raisins

1 onion, chopped fine

1 medium-sized tomato, peeled, chopped and drained

2 cloves garlic, chopped

8 stuffed olives, chopped

12 capers

¾ cup pine nuts

2 tablespoons olive oil

¾ cup fine bread crumbs

4 tablespoons butter

Remove crab meat from shells and wash both well. Chop the crab meat and add it to a sauce which has been made by frying the parsley, almonds, raisins, onion, tomato, garlic, olives, capers and pine nuts together for two or three minutes in the olive oil. Place the mixture in the crab shells. Cover with bread crumbs and bits of butter. Bake in a moderate oven (350 degrees F.) until brown. Yield: six servings.

JAIBAS EN SUS CONCHAS (*Crabs in Shells*)

8 fresh crabs	1 teaspoon capers
½ cup olive oil	1 teaspoon salt
2 cloves garlic, chopped fine	½ teaspoon pepper
1 large onion, chopped fine	1 tablespoon chopped parsley
1 tablespoon cornstarch	
2 large tomatoes, peeled and chopped	24 chopped olives
	½ cup fine dry bread crumbs
2 pimientos, chopped fine	
2 hard-cooked egg yolks	2 ounces grated cheese

Clean crabs well and remove the meat. Wash the shells and let them dry. Heat oil, add garlic and onion, fry till transparent, add cornstarch and cook, stirring till brown. Add crab meat and simmer about ten minutes. Add tomatoes, pimientos, the yolks of eggs, chopped, capers, salt, pepper and parsley and simmer five minutes. Add chopped olives and cook over low heat five minutes. Fill crab shells with the mixture. Cover each with bread crumbs and grated cheese and bake in a moderate oven (350 degrees F.) about fifteen minutes. Serve very hot. Yield: eight servings.

JAIBAS A LA MEXICANA (*Crabs, Mexican-Style*)

18 crabs	½ small onion, chopped
Juice of one lemon	3 eggs, beaten
Salt and pepper	1 small tomato, peeled and chopped
¼ cup butter	
3 tablespoons olive oil	4 tablespoons bread crumbs
1 clove garlic, chopped	4 tablespoons grated cheese

Clean crabs, remove meat (reserving twelve shells) and soak in water with lemon juice and salt for half an hour. Drain. Heat butter with olive oil, add garlic, onion, crab meat, salt and pepper and cook until the meat is golden brown. Add eggs and tomato and fry together three or four minutes. Fill twelve shells and sprinkle tops with bread crumbs and grated cheese. Bake in moderately hot oven (400 degrees F.) ten minutes. Yield: six servings.

LANGOSTA A LA POBLANA (*Puebla-Style Lobster*)

2 two-pound lobsters	½ teaspoon thyme
1 tablespoon salt	½ teaspoon nutmeg
¼ cup olive oil	1 teaspoon pepper
3 tablespoons fat	1 cup brandy
1 onion, chopped	½ cup tomato purée
2 cloves garlic, chopped fine	1 cup stock
1 carrot, boiled and sliced	3 tablespoons chopped
½ teaspoon laurel	parsley
½ teaspoon marjoram	

Boil lobsters in water with two teaspoons salt, eight minutes. Remove, clean and cut in slices. Fry in three tablespoons of oil and three tablespoons fat with onion, garlic, carrot, seasonings and one teaspoon salt. When the lobster takes on a reddish color, remove from heat, pour brandy over it and light. Let burn until sauce has evaporated. Then add tomato purée and bake covered, in a hot oven (425 degrees F.) for twenty minutes. Drain and place lobster in another pan. Strain the sauce over the lobster. Then add stock, remaining oil and simmer another four or five minutes. Serve very hot garnished with parsley. Yield: six servings.

PULPOS EN SU TINTA (*Fresh Octopus in Its Ink*)

3 good-sized octopuses
2 black peppers
2 laurel leaves
¼ cup olive oil
4 cloves garlic, chopped
2 large onions, chopped

1 pound tomatoes, peeled
    and chopped
1 green pepper, chopped
1 tablespoon parsley,
    chopped
⅛ teaspoon allspice

Wash the octopuses well in salted water, place in a towel and beat against the table very hard several times, or hammer it with the edge of a wooden spoon; then wash again in clear water and divide into small portions. Grind the peppers and the laurel leaves. Heat olive oil, add garlic and onions and when they begin to brown, add tomatoes, peppers and parsley. When the mixture starts to boil, add the octopus. Cover the pan and simmer about thirty minutes, then add the rest of the ingredients and the black juice of the octopus. Continue to boil, until octopus is tender. Yield: six servings.

PULPOS EN SU TINTA (*Canned Octopus in Its Ink*)

4 cloves garlic
2 bay leaves
½ cup diced onion
¼ cup diced green pepper
3 tablespoons butter
2 cups canned tomatoes
2 tablespoons chopped
    parsley

Salt and pepper to taste
½ teaspoon allspice
2 cups canned octopus or
    squid with juice
3 cups hot boiled rice

Chop garlic and bay leaves with onion and green pepper. Cook for ten minutes in butter over a low flame. Add tomatoes, parsley, salt, pepper and allspice and cook two or three minutes more or until the mixture has begun to bubble. Add the octopus with its juice and simmer over low heat thirty minutes. Serve very hot with rice. Yield: six servings.

PULPOS A LA MARINERA (*Octopus, Mariner-Style*)

2 one-pound pieces octopus or squid	2 medium-sized onions, chopped
3 tablespoons olive oil	1 cup tomato purée
2 cloves garlic	3 laurel leaves
2 tablespoons chopped parsley	1 teaspoon marjoram
	1 teaspoon thyme

Have octopus or squid cleaned at the market. Remove stones and ink sacs, wash meat thoroughly and cut into small chunks. Fry in oil until outside is browned. Cook in a pressure cooker with two tablespoons water at fifteen pounds pressure for fifteen minutes. Mix together and add the remaining ingredients. Cover cooker and cook ten minutes at fifteen pounds pressure. Yield: six servings.

OSTIONES GUISADOS (*Stewed Oysters*)

3 dozen raw oysters, drained	½ teaspoon pepper
½ sweet pepper, chopped	2 tablespoons olive oil
2 tomatoes, peeled and chopped	1½ tablespoons lemon juice
2 onions, peeled and chopped	12 olives, pitted and chopped
2 cloves garlic, chopped	1 tablespoon capers
2 tablespoons fat	1 tablespoon seedless raisins, .chopped
1 teaspoon salt	2 teaspoons parsley
1 tablespoon vinegar	2 tablespoons bread crumbs

Drain oysters, reserving one and one-half cups liquid. Fry pepper, tomatoes, onions and garlic in the fat five minutes. Add salt, vinegar, pepper, olive oil, lemon juice, olives, capers, raisins and parsley, oysters and juice. Cook over moderate heat in an uncovered pot fifteen minutes or until most of the liquid has evaporated. Serve sprinkled with bread crumbs. Yield: six servings.

OSTIONES A LA VERACRUZANA (*Oysters, Veracruz-Style*)

One of the wonderful things about Mexico is that everywhere it touches the sea. Its geography is bound with miles and miles of palm-fringed coast, each part richer than the other in sea food and coconuts.

Veracruz is the home of shrimp. It is also noted for its oysters. All the little coastal towns of the state have oyster bars where the men in their white guayaberas sit with a glass of beer or mescal into the hot afternoons and the sudden dark. Hundreds of miles away, on the steep plateau of Central Mexico, most little towns and every sizable market boast of stands where the passerby can have ostiones in the Veracruz manner.

Of the innumerable ways of cooking oysters, we have chosen this for you as the very best.

4 dozen oysters	1 tablespoon lard
1 teaspoon salt	1 cup canned tomatoes
4 tablespoons lemon juice	1 tablespoon minced onion
1 teaspoon pepper	1 tablespoon minced parsley
1 teaspoon allspice	4 eggs
¼ cup bread crumbs	3 tablespoons butter

Wash and drain oysters, sprinkle with salt, add lemon juice and let stand. Mix pepper, allspice and bread crumbs. In a saucepan which has been well greased with lard, fry the tomatoes, onion and parsley.

Beat whites of eggs stiffly and add beaten yolks slowly while beating. Grease another pan and spread a layer of the seasoned breadcrumbs on the bottom, then a layer of beaten eggs, then one of oysters, and another of tomato and onion, and finally, another layer of the egg mixture. Repeat this process until all ingredients have been used. Add little chunks of butter and bake in a slow oven (325 degrees F.) until firm or about thirty minutes. Yield: six servings.

REVOLTIJO DE CAMARONES (*Vegetable Stew with Shrimp*)

1 pound cooked shrimp	½ cup rice, washed
2 tablespoons fat	2 ears sweet corn, cut in
2 tablespoons onion,	one-inch lengths
chopped fine	¾ cup peas
2 cloves garlic, chopped fine	½ pound potatoes, peeled
3 tomatoes, broiled, peeled,	and diced
chopped, drained	¾ cup lima beans
1 teaspoon salt	3-ounce package cream
½ teaspoon pepper	cheese, mashed

Peel the shrimp and wash well. Cook in one quart of water about ten minutes. Heat fat, add onion, garlic and tomatoes and fry five minutes over low heat. Add shrimp with one cup of the liquid in which they were cooked, salt, pepper, rice, corn, peas, potatoes and lima beans. Cook, covered, for thirty minutes or until all the vegetables are tender. Add cheese, stir and cook a minute or two longer. Serve as soup, adding water if needed, or serve poured over poached eggs. Yield: six servings.

BUDIN DE CAMARONES (*Shrimp Soufflé*)

Sea food and especially shrimp is enjoyed by the pleasure-loving Mexicans from the North to the Guatemala border. You can eat it in the rough bustle of a Tampico café or more leisurely from ornate bowls full of the rich green sauce of the Yucatecos. One of the happiest ways is at an Isthmus picnic beneath pepper and palm trees, with lovely brown-skinned Tehuantepec women lifting the shrimp from the barbecue pit and handing them delicately roasted to you on a banana leaf plate with large containers of chilled coconut milk.

Here is another way of preparing shrimp; more civilized, but no less flavorful.

½ pound tomatoes, peeled
1 onion
2 tablespoons butter
2 pounds fresh shrimp,
    shelled

Parsley to taste
1 pint light cream
6 eggs

Chop tomatoes and onion and fry in butter. Add shrimp which have been washed and chopped, parsley and cream. Beat separately egg yolks and whites, fold together and add to the shrimp mixture. Pour into a greased pan, set in a pan of hot water, and bake in a moderate oven (350 degrees F.) until firm or about thirty minutes. Yield: six servings.

CAMARONES REALES (*Royal Shrimps*)

1 green pepper, peeled and
    seeded
½ pound mushroom caps,
    cleaned, sliced
3 tablespoons butter
1 small onion, chopped fine
3 tablespoons flour
1 teaspoon salt

3 tablespoons chopped
    pimiento
1 teaspoon chopped parsley
¼ teaspoon Tabasco sauce
2 cups canned or fresh
    cooked shrimps
2 cups milk
1 egg

Dice green pepper and fry with mushrooms in butter five minutes. Add onion, flour, salt, pimiento, parsley, Tabasco and shrimp. Cook over low heat two or three minutes. Then add one and one-half cups milk, stirring, and continue to cook over low heat until the mixture is thick. Add remaining half-cup of milk which has been mixed with the beaten egg. Heat, stirring, and serve on toast. Yield: six to eight servings.

TORTUGA ESTOFADA (*Stewed Turtle*)

¾ pound canned or cooked
   turtle meat
12 capers
8 large green olives
1 tablespoon raisins
⅛ cup almonds
2 tablespoons olive oil
1 medium-sized tomato

2 sweet peppers
1 pimiento
⅛ teaspoon saffron
½ teaspoon allspice
1 teaspoon cinnamon
½ teaspoon cloves
½ cup sherry
Salt and pepper

Place turtle meat in a saucepan and cook about ten minutes. (If fresh turtle is used, wash well and cook thoroughly in salted water before following this procedure.) Add capers, olives, raisins and almonds and set aside. Put one tablespoon olive oil in saucepan and fry briefly chopped tomato, peppers, pimiento, saffron, allspice, cinnamon and cloves. Add to the turtle meat, heat to boiling and add one tablespoon olive oil, sherry and salt and pepper to taste. Cook for five minutes and serve very hot. Yield: six servings.

Chapter 5

Meats

THE AZTECS, the Toltecs, the Mayans, and other indigenous peoples of Mexico had many sophisticated dishes before Cortes and his band of a few hundred arrived at the City of the True Cross on the morning of Good Friday, 1519. They had more after.

Not the least important was the contribution of meat.

It is true that there was infinite variety among the dishes prepared then, but not a single piece of today's favorites—pork, beef, lamb or veal. Until the Spaniards brought in domesticated animals, the principal dishes had been sea food and game in great abundance, then as now. Yucatan is still known as the "land of the pheasant and deer" and both are consumed there with gusto. Venison is a popular dish in the northern states. And, of course, everywhere more exotic dishes are served.

The people of Oaxaca, Guerrero, and Chiapas are partial to iguana—a giant lizard with meat as delicate and fine-flavored as chicken. Iguana roe is a special delicacy. Hunter's Stew often includes armadillo, curassow and whatever else happens to be brought in from the forest or jungle in time for the breakfast pot.

The meats which were the gift of the Spaniards have been adapted to the local cuisine. Most popular is steak. Even in small hotels in villages reached after days on horseback, "filete" or "biftec" (sometimes also called "bistek") is an invariable. So developed has become the cattle industry in the states of the northern plain that even soup of filete is no extravagance.

There are however more elaborate dishes of meat which are scarcely less popular. Veal comes in a variety of forms —veal cutlets, veal southern-style, veal in a rich sauce made of peanuts. Peanuts, incidentally, are indigenous and much used in the preparation of meat dishes and sauces. They help to make up the Mole Poblano.

Various parts of the animals are used, with kidneys (invariably wined), liver and brains most common. Pig's feet are a special delicacy cooked with milk and raisins, and even the skin is utilized in the crisp delicious chicharron, which is like southern cracklings but acquires zest from the admixture of chili powder or hot spicy sauce.

Since shortly after that Good Friday in 1519, no main meal, except during the Lenten fasting season, has been complete without meat for those able to afford it—happily, an ever-increasing number. And, all the familiar ways of preparing it prevail: meat balls, roasts, hash, deviled meat, jellied meat "cheeses," meat with sauce and meat without. But no matter in what form it comes, it is always—like Mexico—"familiar as home, but different and exciting."

Meat is frequently part of antojitos: tamales of the more substantial variety, tacos, tortas and tostadas. Every market in the city and country has large stalls where pieces of meat are sold and nearby is the "tortilla woman," with great stacks of corn wafers covered with a napkin and waiting to be sold. This meat is barbacoa.

"Barbacoa—domingos y festivos" is a sign which appears with surprising frequency in rustic restaurants outside of the capital and other large cities. And barbecue in the Mexican manner is truly a Sunday and holiday affair. Barbecues vary from region to region, but the particular preparation which has achieved most fame is that of the State of Mexico, the maguey-growing region around the Federal District. Only two things are necessary for a barbecue: meat, preferably mutton, and "sufficient maguey leaves." Other desirable requirements are a lovely wooded picnicking spot near a colonial convent or a pre-Conquest archaeological zone; an entire day to spend in the country and some pleasant friends; a guitar for singing and some pulque for the sauce and for immediate pleasure.

The approved method of pit barbecuing any meat requires time and endurance—but the compensations are great. In Oaxaca and other areas where a barbecue is a traditional way of celebrating any major event, things get under way the evening before the feast. A large square hole about three feet deep is dug; porous rocks are placed on the bottom on top of which are piled kindling and logs. The fire is lighted at midnight or shortly after and is allowed to burn through the night.

The next morning, the embers and glowing logs are removed. Huge *cazuelas* of rice and sometimes corn are placed on the rocks. The meat, that has been prepared for roasting, is placed on top of the uncovered *cazuelas*. Maguey leaves are stuck into the earth so that the sides of the pit are completely lined with them, and the tops are bent over to form a cover for the meat. A metal shield is placed on top of the pit to protect the barbecue, the four sides of which are weighted with stones. Although the intense heat stored in the rocks and in the earth walls of the pit is usually enough to cook the meat, frequently a bonfire is built on top of the metal cover—which has been buried under several inches of earth. The fire is kept burning for about eight hours.

Then the earth is shoveled off the metal shield and the weights are removed. The pit is uncovered, the leaves pulled back, and the meat and other ingredients are removed and served.

Other, less elaborate forms of barbecuing are also popular. The next time you plan a barbecue—outdoors or in your apartment—if you have a charcoal brazier or a Japanese hibachi grill, you might try *carne asada,* a simply prepared, delicious beef dish that is a favorite at any time and in almost any place. Slice a cut of beef into long, thin strips: about two inches by four and about a quarter of an inch thick. Lay the strips of meat on the glowing coals of the barbecue until they begin to sizzle; turn, and cook the other side. The meat may be served sandwich-style, folded into a tortilla spread with guacamole, or more formally, with beans or rice and vegetables, as a main dish.

For those who prefer to spend the day in the country hiking or climbing pyramids, all of the markets in the Valley sell barbecue for rolling in tortillas and eating when and where the fancy moves.

In leisurely Tehuantepec a simpler method of cooking meat has been evolved. While the men relax beneath a mango tree or go expeditioning for papayas and bananas, the women build a roaring fire. When the fire has burned down, they roast the dried meat, fish and shrimps on the embers. In the North, kid—a popular dish—is prepared "al pastor" which means that it, or any other meat, is hung over a bonfire and cooked as the shepherds cook.

Even in remote regions, where Spanish is rarely heard and where the tribal occupations of fishing and hunting still constitute men's work, meat-eating is characteristic of fiesta. Everyday food in the Popoluca country consists of eggs, tortillas and coffee and occasionally fried bananas, but no fiesta would be complete without the sacrifice of a pig or a cow. Sponsoring a fiesta is a serious matter in the Popoluca country as elsewhere. To be selected sponsor implies that a man has community standing and has property and reputation. For the fiesta to be successful, there must be fireworks and gaiety and plenty of meat and tamales for all. And, if it is successful, well—that is the ultimate that can happen to a a man.

FILETES COMPUESTOS (*Beef Fillets*)

6 slices fillet of beef	Pinch of salt and pepper
2 tablespoons lemon juice	6 slices toast
3 tablespoons olive oil	¼ cup grated cheese
3 tablespoons shortening	18 stuffed olives, sliced
1 teaspoon marjoram	2 canned chilpotles, sliced
½ teaspoon thyme	(Page 238)

Sprinkle steaks with lemon juice and let stand ten minutes. Fry in hot olive oil and shortening till brown. Mix marjoram, thyme, salt and pepper and sprinkle over steaks. Place each steak on a piece of toast in a pan, sprinkle with grated cheese, olives and chilpotles and heat under the broiler for one or two minutes. Yield: six servings.

BIFTEC LUCIA (*Beefsteak Lucia*)

6 steaks, half inch thick
1 teaspoon salt
1 teaspoon pepper
½ cup flour
6 tablespoons butter
½ pound fresh mushrooms, sliced
¼ cup rum

½ cup boiling water
½ cup white wine
½ teaspoon nutmeg
2 tablespoons tomato paste or purée
½ teaspoon sugar
1 cup cream

Sprinkle steaks with salt and pepper and dredge with flour. Fry in butter until they are done to taste. Remove. In the same butter, fry the mushrooms until golden and tender. Put the steaks back in the pan with the mushrooms, pour rum over them and light. When the rum has burned out, add boiling water, white wine and nutmeg. Cover, and simmer eight to ten minutes. Add tomato paste or purée and sugar. Cook five minutes longer and add cream just before serving. Yield: six servings.

BIFTEC DE POBRE (*Beefsteak of the Poor*)

1½ pounds ground beef
½ pound ground pork
1½ teaspoons salt, approximately
½ teaspoon pepper
½ cup fat

1 large tomato, peeled, chopped and drained
2 cloves garlic, chopped fine
1 teaspoon chili powder
¼ teaspoon cumin

Mix beef and pork with salt and pepper and form into tiny thin cakes, like small hamburgers. Fry in hot fat until well cooked. Remove. Mix tomato, garlic, chili powder and cumin and fry in the fat in which the meat was fried. Add one-half cup of water and salt to taste and simmer for five minutes. Serve with Pickled Sauce (Page 62). Yield: six to eight servings.

BIFTEC A LA MEXICANA (*Mexican Beefsteak*)

1 cup small red beans
½ cup shortening
1 cup cream
6 tender four-ounce
    beefsteaks

2 tablespoons butter
1 teaspoon salt
⅛ teaspoon pepper

Soak the beans two hours in water to cover and cook, covered, till soft. Drain, grind and fry in shortening. Butter six individual baking dishes and put a layer of beans in the bottom of each. Add a thin layer of cream. Top with steaks, spread with butter and sprinkle with salt and pepper. Bake in a moderately hot oven (400 degrees F.) until steaks are tender. Yield: six servings.

CARNE EN BRAZO CON SALSA (*Meat Roll with Sauce*)

1 pound any tender meat,
    ground
½ teaspoon pepper
1 teaspoon salt
1 tablespoon vinegar
2 hard-cooked eggs
3 medium-sized tomatoes,
    peeled

1 medium-sized onion,
    chopped
1 tablespoon shortening
1 sweet pepper, peeled and
    chopped
1 teaspoon Tabasco sauce

Mix meat, pepper, salt and vinegar. Spread meat on a napkin and place the hard-cooked eggs in the center. Roll tightly, tying the napkin at both ends so that it does not loosen. Place on the rack of a pressure cooker and cook for twenty minutes at 15 pounds pressure. If double boiler is used, cooking time is about two hours. Remove the meat roll from the napkin and place it on a platter. Before serving pour over it the following sauce: Chop tomatoes and drain. Fry onion in shortening until lightly browned. Add tomatoes, sweet pepper and Tabasco and simmer five minutes. Yield: six servings.

CARNE DE RES DE MAZATLAN
(*Beef, Mazatlan-Style, with Sauce*)

2 pounds lean sirloin steak	2 tablespoons butter
1 teaspoon salt	2 tablespoons olive oil
½ teaspoon pepper	6 slices toast

Cut the meat into six equal strips and sprinkle salt and pepper on both sides. Heat butter and olive oil in a frying pan, put in steaks and cook over high heat four minutes on each side. Place each fillet on a slice of toast and cover with the following sauce:

Sauce

3 tablespoons butter	2 tablespoons flour
1 tablespoon olive oil	3 cups tomato purée
1 carrot, sliced	1 teaspoon chili powder
1 clove garlic, ground	½ teaspoon salt
1 onion, chopped	1 green pepper, chopped
2 teaspoons parsley, chopped	1 pimiento, chopped
1 laurel leaf, finely chopped	

Heat two tablespoons butter and the olive oil in a frying pan. Add carrot, garlic, onion, parsley and laurel and cook over moderate heat three or four minutes, until onion is browned. Then add flour and stir until flour is golden brown. Add tomato purée, chili, salt, green pepper and pimiento and let simmer thirty minutes. Just before pouring over fillets add one tablespoon butter. Yield: six servings.

CARNE DE RES CON SALSA DE PASAS
(*Beef with Raisin Sauce*)

2 pounds tender beef
4 ounces ham
6 cloves garlic
2 tablespoons shortening
1 teaspoon salt
⅛ teaspoon marjoram

2 tablespoons butter
½ cup raisins
3 medium-sized tomatoes
12 olives
2 canned chilies Jalapeños
  (Page 238)

Using a sharp knife make small deep incisions in the meat and stuff with strips of ham and slices of garlic. Fry in shortening until lightly browned. Add water to cover meat, salt and marjoram and simmer slowly thirty minutes. Heat butter in a frying pan and fry raisins with tomatoes which have been peeled, chopped and drained. Slice meat and cover with sauce. Garnish with olives and chilies. Yield: six servings.

ALBONDIGAS (*Meat Balls*)

1 pound beef, ground
½ pound pork, ground
1 slice bread, crumbled
¼ cup rice, washed
1 egg, beaten
1 clove garlic, chopped
Dash each of black sage,
  ground mint and pepper

1 teaspoon salt
⅛ teaspoon cilantro
  (or use chopped parsley)
2 tablespoons fat
1 onion, chopped
1 tomato, peeled and
  mashed

Mix meats with bread which has been soaked in water and squeezed. Add rice, egg and seasonings. Mold into balls the size of walnuts. Heat fat, sauté onion, remove and fry meat balls until browned. Add onion, tomato and duplicates of the same spices which were mixed with the meat. Add four cups of boiling water and simmer slowly for one and one-half hours. Yield: six servings.

ASADO (*Roast*)

1½ pounds round or chuck steak	1 cup cooked peas
1 onion, sliced	1 cup cooked string beans, sliced
4 tablespoons butter	3 avocados, peeled and sliced
1 cup stock	
½ cup red wine	½ cup mayonnaise
2 laurel leaves	1 teaspoon salt
2 raw carrots, grated	¼ teaspoon pepper

Brown meat and onion in butter. Add stock and cook fifteen minutes. Add wine and laurel and simmer one hour or until meat is tender.

Prepare following salad: Mix vegetables, add mayonnaise and salt and pepper to taste. Place meat in the center of serving dish and surround with the salad. Yield: six servings.

CHORIZOS (*Mexican Sausage*)

3 pounds pork	2 tablespoons salt
12 chilies anchos, peeled and seeded (Page 238)	2 cloves garlic
1 tablespoon pepper	1 cup vinegar
½ teaspoon cumin	5 yards of cleaned sausage casing

Cut meat into tiny pieces and place in a deep bowl. Soak chilies in enough water to cover for ten minutes. Drain and grind with pepper, cumin, salt and garlic. Mix with diced meat. Add vinegar and mix well, with hands. Allow mixture to stand twenty-four hours in a cool place or in refrigerator.

Clean and wash sausage casings very well in water and then in vinegar. Stuff with the prepared mixture, making each sausage about four inches in length by tying each with dried corn leaves cut in strips or with cord. Make several pin pricks in each sausage to allow air to escape. Dry in the sun for at least four days. Yield: about three pounds.

CARNE MANCHA MANTELES (*"Tablecloth Stainers"*)

2 pounds pork meat
4 dried red chilies (Page 238)
4 medium-sized tomatoes, peeled, chopped and drained
3 tablespoons fat
1 teaspoon salt
¼ teaspoon cloves
½ teaspoon powdered cinnamon
¼ teaspoon cumin
1 medium-sized onion, quartered
¼ teaspoon orégano
1 teaspoon sugar
2 sweet potatoes, cooked and sliced
2 apples, peeled, cored and sliced
2 bananas, sliced
2 slices pineapple

Simmer pork in two cups of water until tender. Remove seeds from chilies, toast them lightly over flame, taking care not to burn, and soak in cold water about ten minutes. Drain and chop. Fry chilies and tomatoes in the fat five minutes. Add the stock in which pork was cooked, salt, cloves, cinnamon, cumin, onion and orégano and the meat which has been diced. Cook over low heat about ten minutes. Add sugar, sweet potatoes, apples, bananas and pineapple and cook over low heat ten minutes longer. Yield: six servings.

LOMO EN SALSA DE RAJAS (*Pork Loin with Pepper Sauce*)

3 cloves garlic
1 Mexican sausage
2 tablespoons shortening
2 pounds pork loin
1 onion, peeled and chopped
4 large tomatoes, peeled
1 quart stock
1 teaspoon salt
4 sweet peppers, peeled and sliced
3 avocados

Fry garlic and sausage in shortening and remove. Brown pork in the same fat. Add half of the onion, two chopped tomatoes, fried garlic and sausage, stock and salt. Simmer about thirty minutes or until meat is soft and the sauce thick. Remove meat and slice. Fry peppers and other half of onion and pour over meat. Garnish with slices of remaining two tomatoes and avocados. Yield: six servings.

PICADILLO (*Chopped Meat*)

1 pound pork meat, chopped	2 onions
1 pound veal, chopped	½ cup olives
1 tablespoon sugar	1 tablespoon capers
Salt and pepper	¼ cup almonds
2 cloves garlic	¼ cup raisins
2 medium-sized tomatoes, peeled	

Place pork, veal, sugar, salt and pepper in kettle, and add boiling water to barely cover meat. Cover pot and simmer one hour. Remove cover and cook until water has evaporated. Chop garlic, tomatoes and onions and fry seven or eight minutes. Before mixture has dried, add olives, capers, almonds and the raisins which have been washed and chopped. Yield: six servings.

CARNE ENDIABLADA (*Deviled Meat*)

1 pound pork loin, ground	4 soda crackers, crumbled
½ cup ground ham	½ teaspoon nutmeg
2 strips bacon, ground	½ teaspoon pepper
2 eggs	1 teaspoon salt

Mix together all ingredients and knead thoroughly. Wrap in heavy greased paper or parchment and cook in a covered double boiler for one hour. Yield: six servings.

ALBONDIGON (*Spiced Meat Loaf*)

1 pound chopped beef	2 raw eggs
1 pound chopped pork	1 onion, chopped
1 slice boiled ham	Salt, pepper, orégano
½ loaf bread, crumbled	½ cup sherry wine
and soaked in milk	3 hard-cooked eggs

Grind beef, pork and ham together. Mix with bread, raw eggs, onion, salt, pepper, orégano and sherry. Mold the mixture into a loaf with the hard-cooked eggs in the center and wrap in a damp cloth, fastening both ends. Bake in a moderate oven (350 degrees F.) for one and one-half hours, basting from time to time with pan drippings. Cool and slice. Yield: eight to ten servings.

CARNERO RAMONA (*Mutton Ramona*)

2 pounds leg of mutton	1 laurel leaf
5 thin slices boiled ham	1 teaspoon marjoram
4 cloves garlic	½ teaspoon thyme
1 tablespoon lard	3 medium-sized tomatoes
1 carrot, sliced	1 pint boiling water
1 medium-sized onion,	Salt and pepper to taste
sliced	

Insert knife at intervals in the mutton and stuff the holes with small pieces of ham and tiny slices of garlic. Brown meat in lard. Remove from pan and place in kettle. Using the same pan, fry carrot, onion, laurel, marjoram and thyme until golden brown. Pour off excess fat, add tomatoes, peeled and sliced, and fry five minutes. Pour mixture over meat, cover, and cook over low heat, stirring often, thirty minutes. Add boiling water, salt and pepper and allow to simmer four hours over very low heat. Add water as needed. Yield: six servings.

COSTILLAS DE PUERCO (*Mexican-Style Pork Ribs*)

2 tablespoons vinegar	1 large onion
2 pounds pork ribs	6 sprigs cilantro (or use
Salt	parsley)
6 dried black peppers	1 teaspoon black pepper
4 large tomatoes	

Rub vinegar into pork, sprinkle with salt and let stand in a glass baking dish one hour. Peel and chop peppers, tomatoes and onion. Add cilantro or parsley, black pepper and a few teaspoons of water. Pour sauce over meat. Bake in a moderate oven (350 degrees F.) one and one-half hours. Serve with guacamole. (Page 59). Yield: six servings.

CARNE OAXAQHEÑA (*Oaxaca Meat Dish with Chochoyotes*)

½ cup white beans	1 small onion, chopped
1 frying chicken	2 cloves garlic, chopped
1 pound pork meat, diced	3 small green peppers,
1 pint hot water	chopped
½ teaspoon salt	1 tablespoon cilantro
¼ cup string beans	(optional)
¼ cup zucchini, diced	1 sprig parsley, chopped
1 cup tomato purée	2 tablespoons fat

Soak beans overnight and boil one hour or until tender. Drain and put in a kettle with chicken and pork which have been cut into small portions. Add hot water and simmer fifteen minutes. Add salt and simmer until chicken is almost cooked. Add string beans and zucchini and cook fifteen minutes.

Fry tomato purée, onion, garlic, green peppers, cilantro and parsley in fat five minutes. Add to the chicken. Then add chochoyotes and simmer twenty minutes. Sprinkle with parsley before serving. Yield: six servings.

Chochoyotes

6 tortillas   1 teaspoon salt
½ cup fat

Soak tortillas in enough water to cover until very soft,
drain and grind. Mix with fat and salt, and beat well. Form
into small balls, size of pecans. Yield: six servings.

TORTA AZTECA (*Aztec-Style Loaf*)

2 pounds pork meat, cubed   4 small sweet peppers,
½ cup shortening   shredded
1 clove garlic, ground   4 eggs, separated
1 large onion, chopped   8 six-inch tortillas
4 tomatoes, peeled, chopped   ½ cup butter
   and drained   1 cup grated cheese

Fry pork thoroughly in two tablespoons shortening and
grind. In the rest of the shortening fry garlic, onion and
tomatoes for about five minutes. Add one-half cup water,
peppers and the meat. Beat egg whites, then yolks and fold
together. Fry the tortillas in butter until lightly browned and
dip in beaten eggs. Butter a glass baking dish and place two
of the tortillas in it. Spread with a layer of the meat mixture
and a layer of the grated cheese. Repeat layer until ingredients have been used. Bake in a hot oven (425 degrees F.)
ten minutes. Yield: six servings.

ALMENDRADO (*Meat with Almond Sauce*)

2 pounds pork or veal loin   1 slice white bread,
1 onion, chopped   crumbled
4 tomatoes, peeled and   ½ teaspoon cinnamon
   chopped   Salt
3 tablespoons fat   1 pound small potatoes,
1 cup almonds, blanched   cooked
   and fried   10 sweet pickles
4 whole black peppers

Simmer meat in water to cover until tender, drain and slice. Fry onion and tomatoes in two tablespoons hot fat four minutes, add almonds and peppers. Cool and grind to a smooth paste. Add bread, cinnamon and salt to taste. Fry again in the remaining fat. Cool and grind again. Simmer mixture with sliced meat and two cups of stock ten to twelve minutes or until the sauce is thick. Garnish with cooked potatoes and sweet pickles if desired. Yield: six servings.

LOMO EN AVELLANAS (*Meat in Hazelnut Sauce*)

½ pound pork loin, ground	2 laurel leaves
1 pound veal, ground	½ teaspoon thyme
8 olives, chopped	½ teaspoon marjoram
1 medium-sized onion, chopped	1 tablespoon cornstarch
	3 tablespoons butter
2 pickled peppers, chopped	1⅓ cups hazelnuts, blanched and ground
2 raw eggs	
1 teaspoon salt	1 cup stock
½ teaspoon pepper	½ cup dry sherry wine
2 hard-cooked eggs	1 cup cooked peas, strained

Mix meats with olives, onion, pickled peppers, raw eggs, salt and pepper. Spread out on a damp napkin. Place the two hard-cooked eggs in the center and roll meat round them. Fasten napkin ends. Cook in a covered pot in two cups of water with herbs for two hours. Cool and unwrap.

Brown cornstarch in two tablespoons butter, add hazelnuts, stock, pepper and salt to taste. Cook over moderate heat until the sauce begins to thicken. Add sherry. Put the meat roll in the sauce and cook over low heat until the sauce begins to boil. Melt remaining butter in a frying pan, add and heat pea purée. Place meat on a serving dish, pour sauce over it and place purée around edge of meat. Yield: six servings.

MOCHOMOS (*Shredded Pork Meat*)

1½ pounds pork meat   1 teaspoon salt

Cook pork in two cups water thirty minutes or until all
the water has evaporated. Grind meat, add salt and fry it
in its own fat, if necessary add one teaspoon of shortening,
until a golden brown. Serve on a hot platter surrounded by
Guacamole (Page 59). Yield: six servings.

LOMO DE PUERCO EN CERVEZA (*Pork Loin with Beer*)

2 pounds pork loin   1 tablespoon shortening
1 teaspoon salt   ½ pint beer
⅛ teaspoon pepper   1 tablespoon sugar

Sprinkle meat with salt and pepper and fry in shortening
until brown. Add beer in which sugar has been dissolved.
When the beer takes on a dark golden color, add three-
quarters cup water and simmer twenty minutes. Add a little
more water as needed. Slice meat before serving. Yield: six
servings.

TINGA POBLANA (*Hash, Puebla-Style*)

2 pounds pork loin   1 canned chilpotle, shredded
1 tablespoon salt   (Page 238)
2 tablespoons fat   ½ teaspoon orégano
2 onions   1 avocado, sliced
1 clove garlic, chopped   ¼ cup vinegar
4 large tomatoes, peeled,
   chopped and drained

Simmer pork in two cups water with two teaspoons salt
one hour. Remove, reserving stock. Cool meat and shred.
Heat fat, add one onion, chopped, and the garlic and fry

until the onion is transparent. Add tomatoes and simmer eight minutes. Add the shredded meat and one-half cup reserved stock and simmer until the mixture begins to thicken. Add the chilpotle and orégano and simmer two or three minutes longer. Garnish with avocado and one onion which has been sliced and allowed to stand fifteen minutes in one-half cup water, the vinegar and one teaspoon salt. Yield: six servings.

POZOLE DE GUADALAJARA (*Pork with Hominy*)

½ pound pig's head	2 pigs feet, cooked and
2 pounds pork loin, cut into	boned
small pieces	2 teaspoons chili powder
1 four-pound roaster	1 teaspoon salt
1½ cups hominy	1 teaspoon chopped garlic

Boil the pig's head, pork loin, hominy and pig's feet in one cup of water, covered, one-half hour. Cook with those ingredients the roaster, which has been cut in serving-sized portions. Add water if needed. Add the chili powder, salt and garlic and simmer one hour or until meat is very tender. Yield: eight servings.

This dish, very popular in the north of Mexico, is always served with the following side dish:

Side Dish

1 small head lettuce,	1 teaspoon orégano
chopped	4 tortillas, cut into small
3 ounces cream cheese,	squares and toasted
sliced	

Mix lettuce and cheese and add orégano. Serve on one side of salad plates with toasted tortilla wedges on the other side.

COSTILLAS EMPAPELADAS (*Veal Chops in Paper*)

6 veal chops	3 tablespoons bread crumbs
¼ cup olive oil	¼ teaspoon laurel
2 tablespoons vinegar	¼ teaspoon marjoram
½ pound boiled ham, ground	¼ teaspoon thyme
	1 teaspoon salt

Fry the chops in oil until tender and golden brown. Remove, add vinegar and cover each chop with a spoonful of the following mixture: ham, bread crumbs, laurel, marjoram, thyme and salt, ground together. Pour the oil and vinegar in the pan over the filling. Wrap each chop in oiled paper and bake in a moderate oven (350 degrees F.) till tender, about forty minutes. Serve with any salad. Yield: six servings.

CHULETAS RELLENAS (*Stuffed Veal Chops*)

6 veal chops, about three-fourth inch thick	Salt
6 hard-cooked egg yolks	1 cup dry white wine
¼ cup grated cheese	2 large onions, sliced thin
¼ cup butter	1 laurel leaf
1¼ teaspoons pepper, approximately	2 cloves
	1 teaspoon marjoram

Slit each chop with a sharp knife so that a pocket is formed. Mix egg yolks with grated cheese, butter and pepper to form a paste. Rub chops with salt and pepper on the outside and moisten inside well with wine. Stuff with egg paste and fasten edges together with picks. Fry together onions, laurel, cloves and marjoram and add chops, the rest of the wine and one-fourth cup water. Cover and simmer slowly for one to one and one-half hours. Serve chops very hot with the sauce. Yield: six servings.

TERNERA EN NOGADA (*Veal in Nut Sauce*)

3 pounds boned rump or
    shoulder of veal
1 large onion
2 cloves garlic
¼ tablespoon thyme
1 teaspoon salt

1 teaspoon pepper
2 tablespoons butter
1 cup pecans, chopped
½ cup cream
1 pint stock

Simmer veal in four cups water with one-half of the onion, the garlic and thyme and one-half the salt and pepper till tender, about two hours. Cool and cut into thin strips. Heat butter in a frying pan, add other half onion, chopped fine, and sauté until transparent. Add pecans, cream, remaining salt and pepper and the stock. Boil, stirring constantly five or six minutes or until the mixture has thickened slightly. Add meat and simmer another five minutes. Yield: six servings.

TERNERA EN SALSA DE CACAHUATE (*Veal in Peanut Sauce*)

2 pounds veal
½ cup shortening
2 cloves garlic
1 onion, finely chopped
4 medium-sized tomatoes

1½ cups peanuts, blanched
3 sprigs parsley
2 cups stock
1 teaspoon salt
¼ teaspoon pepper

Cut veal into small portions and brown in shortening. Add garlic, onion and tomatoes which have been peeled and drained. Cook until almost dry and add peanuts which have been ground with parsley. Brown, and add stock, salt and pepper. Cook over a very slow fire, adding a little water as necessary, for twenty-five minutes or until meat is very tender. Sauce should be as thick as custard. Yield: six servings.

TERNERA ESTILO DEL SUR (*Veal, Southern-Style*)

1 pound veal, sliced	4 cloves garlic, diced
1 teaspoon salt	1 sweet pepper, chopped
¾ cup stock	1 onion, chopped
¼ teaspoon pepper	3 medium-sized tomatoes
¼ teaspoon marjoram	2 sprigs parsley
1 pinch cumin seed	2 tablespoons shortening
1 pinch saffron	3 hard-cooked egg yolks
1 pinch cilantro (optional)	1 tablespoon butter
1 pinch cloves	1 tablespoon vinegar

Pound each slice of meat well. Place in kettle and sprinkle with salt. Add one-half cup stock, herbs, cloves and one clove of garlic. Simmer fifteen minutes. Fry sweet pepper, onion, tomatoes, three cloves of garlic and parsley in the shortening. Add mixture to meat and simmer until tender and almost dry. Blend remaining stock with sieved egg yolks. Add to meat with butter, vinegar, and salt to taste. Boil about eight minutes. Yield: four servings.

TERNERA TRUFADA (*Veal with Truffles*)

1 pound veal loin or cutlet, one-quarter inch thick	1 tablespoon cracker crumbs
	3 ounces ham, ground
½ pound ground veal	2 strips bacon, chopped
4 truffles, chopped	1 medium-sized onion, quartered
1 egg	
2 cups dry white wine	1 laurel leaf
3 teaspoons salt	1 sprig parsley
Pinch of pepper	1 teaspoon marjoram

Remove any fat and sinew from veal and reserve. Spread out on a napkin. Mix together the ground veal, truffles, egg, half of the wine, one teaspoon salt, pepper and crumbs. Spread a layer of this mixture on the veal and add a layer of ham and bacon. Cover with another layer of the veal mixture.

Roll, wrap in the napkin and tie at the ends. Place in a pot with enough water to cover. Add the rest of the wine, onion, herbs, two teaspoons salt and fat and sinews that were removed from the veal. Simmer slowly for one hour or until stock has almost evaporated. Drain and allow to stand for several hours after the napkin has been tightly squeezed to remove excess moisture. Chill and slice before serving. Yield: six servings.

SESOS EN MANTEQUILLA (Brains Cooked in Butter)

2 calves' brains	⅛ teaspoon marjoram
2 cloves garlic	¼ cup butter
2 teaspoons salt	4 sprigs parsley, chopped
1 teaspoon pepper	½ cup vinegar
2 laurel leaves	

Wash the brains and remove membranes. Simmer twenty minutes in water to cover with garlic, half the salt and pepper, the laurel and marjoram. Drain and keep warm. Heat butter with remaining salt, pepper and parsley until the butter is a rich brown color, or for about five minutes. Remove from fire, add vinegar. Boil two minutes. Pour over brains. Yield: six servings.

SESOS LAMPREADOS (Brains with Wine Gravy)

2 pork or calves' brains	Fat for deep frying
1 tablespoon salt	1 large onion, chopped
1 tablespoon lemon juice	1 clove garlic, chopped
3 eggs, separated	1 cup tomato purée
4 tablespoons flour	Salt and pepper to taste

Wash brains in salted cold water. Cover with fresh water, add salt and lemon juice and let stand about half an hour. Remove membranes and drain. Cover again with slightly salted water and simmer fifteen to twenty minutes. Drain and slice. Beat egg whites stiffly and mix with beaten yolks.

Sprinkle slices of brains with flour and dip into the beaten eggs. Fry in deep hot fat (360 degrees F.) until golden brown. Fry onion in a small amount of fat until it begins to brown. Add garlic and tomato purée, salt and pepper and simmer eight minutes. Add brain slices to the sauce and cook one minute longer. Yield: six servings.

RIÑONES CON VINO (*Kidneys with Wine*)

2 beef kidneys	1 tablespoon flour
½ cup vinegar	1 tablespoon fat
1 teaspoon salt	1 cup red wine
1 teaspoon pepper	1 laurel leaf
1 medium-sized onion,	½ teaspoon marjoram
chopped	½ teaspoon thyme

With a sharp knife, cut each kidney into six crosswise slices. Free meat of all gristle and fat. Soak in vinegar with salt and pepper one hour. Fry onion and flour in fat until flour browns. Remove onion from pan and put in the sliced kidneys with half of the vinegar in which they were soaked. Add wine, laurel, marjoram and thyme and simmer, covered, fifteen to twenty minutes. Serve sauce over kidneys. They are usually served with white rice. Yield: six servings.

HIGADO (*Liver*)

6 liver steaks, quarter-inch thick	1 teaspoon salt
	½ teaspoon pepper
5 tablespoons butter	2 pickled peppers, cut into
2 tablespoons lemon juice	small pieces
2 teaspoons parsley, chopped fine	3 toasted tortillas (bought)

Fry the liver in three tablespoons butter about three minutes on each side. Place on platter and spread with the rest of the butter. Sprinkle with lemon juice, parsley, salt and pepper. Pour sauce left in the frying pan over liver. Garnish with pickled peppers and tortillas, cut into squares. Yield: six servings.

HIGADO EN SALSA BLANCA (*Liver in White Sauce*)

1½ pounds beef or pork liver
2 teaspoons butter
2 eggs, beaten
1 teaspoon lemon juice
2 tablespoons flour

½ teaspoon orégano
1 teaspoon salt
½ teaspoon pepper
½ teaspoon nutmeg
2 tablespoons fat

Wash liver, snip out any membranes and dry. Grind and mix with butter, eggs, lemon juice, flour and seasoning and place in the greased top of a double boiler. Cook, covered, forty-five or fifty minutes. Remove from heat and cool. Turn out and cut into slices one-quarter inch thick. Fry slices in fat and cover with the following sauce:

Sauce

1 small onion
½ sweet green pepper
2 sprigs parsley

3 tablespoons fat
3 tablespoons flour
1 cup milk

Chop onion, pepper and parsley and sauté in fat until tender. Blend flour with milk, add and simmer over low heat for five minutes stirring constantly. Yield: six servings.

HIGADO ENVINADO (*Liver with White Wine*)

6 slices liver, half-inch thick
¼ cup butter
1 medium-sized onion, finely chopped
1 clove garlic, finely chopped

1 tablespoon flour
1 cup white wine
1 sprig parsley
2 tablespoons lemon juice

Brown liver quickly in three tablespoons butter. Remove from pan and keep warm. Heat remaining butter in pan and fry onion and garlic until brown. Blend in flour, add wine and stir till thickened. Replace liver, reheat, but do not let sauce boil. Add chopped parsley and lemon juice. Yield: six servings.

LENGUA ALMENDRADA (*Tongue with Almond Sauce*)

2-pound beef tongue	1 teaspoon laurel
6 tablespoons lemon juice	10 black peppers
3 carrots, sliced	6 cloves
1 teaspoon marjoram	1 onion, sliced
1 teaspoon thyme	1 tablespoon salt

Wash tongue well and pound to tenderize. Let stand in enough water to cover with two tablespoons lemon juice for three hours. Drain and put in clear water with two tablespoons lemon juice and let stand for another three hours. Remove and place in a pot with four quarts of water and remaining ingredients. Cook very slowly for eight hours or till tender. Peel off skin and slice. Put slices on a platter and cover with almond sauce prepared as follows:

Almond Sauce

3 sprigs parsley	¾ cup blanched almonds
4 hard-cooked eggs	4 tablespoons olive oil
3 cloves garlic	1 tablespoon vinegar
4 large tomatoes, chopped and drained	Salt and pepper

Grind parsley, egg yolks, garlic, tomatoes and almonds. Simmer ten minutes over low heat until tomato liquid has evaporated. Then add the egg whites, which have been chopped, the olive oil and vinegar. Add salt and pepper to taste. Garnish platter with lettuce and radishes. Yield: six servings.

LENGUA TRUFADA (*Tongue Stuffed with Truffles*)

3 or four pound tongue	½ cup cooked pork meat,
2 sour oranges	chopped
4 truffles	2 eggs
2 teaspoons pepper	¾ cup sherry wine
½ teaspoon nutmeg	2 laurel leaves
3 teaspoons salt	½ teaspoon marjoram
2 slices boiled ham, chopped	2 tablespoons fat

Wash tongue (if it is not a mild cure, soak two hours in enough water to cover and drain). Soak for five minutes in the juice of sour oranges. Drain. Bore a wide hole with a sharp knife through the tongue lengthwise, almost to the tip. Stuff with one truffle which has been ground with one teaspoon pepper, nutmeg and one teaspoon salt. Mix ham and pork and chill for a few minutes. Add remaining pepper, one teaspoon salt, eggs, the rest of the truffles which have been cut into small pieces and one-quarter cup sherry. Mix well and stuff the tongue, taking care to insure that stuffing almost reaches the tip. Sew the opening. Place in a covered pot with one-half cup sherry, one pint water, two teaspoons salt, the laurel and marjoram and simmer about three hours. (Allow forty-five to fifty minutes per pound.) Cool and drain. Fry in fat until outside is brown. Remove and chill. Serve sliced with salad. Yield: ten servings.

MONDONGO (*Tripe*)

1½ pounds tripe	3 large tomatoes, peeled
2½ quarts salted water	6 peppers
½ cup corn kernels	1 banana
2 laurel leaves	2 cloves
1 clove garlic	1 teaspoon paprika
1 large onion	½ teaspoon saffron
1 tablespoon coarse salt	12 leaves of coriander (or
6 tablespoons olive oil	use parsley)

Wash tripe in boiling water and scrape with a knife. Simmer one hour in salted water with corn, laurel, garlic, onion and coarse salt. Fry in olive oil eight to ten minutes chopped tomatoes, peppers, banana, cloves, paprika and saffron. Add to tripe, cover and simmer one hour or until tender. Add coriander or parsley. Yield: six servings.

MONDONGO RANCHERO (*Tripe, Rancher-Style*)

1 pound tripe, cooked
2 cloves garlic, chopped fine
2 onions, chopped fine
3 medium-sized tomatoes, peeled, drained
2 chilies anchos, pitted, soaked and ground (Page 238)
1 teaspoon marjoram
½ teaspoon thyme
1 clove
½ teaspoon pepper
2 teaspoons salt
2 teaspoons parsley, chopped
3 tablespoons olive oil
2 potatoes, cooked and cut into pieces
2 pickled chilies, sliced
20 olives

Fry all but the last three ingredients together in the olive oil for five minutes. Cut tripe into small pieces and add to the mixture with the potatoes. Simmer for about eight minutes. Garnish with chilies and olives. Yield: four servings.

QUESO DE LIEBRE (*Rabbit Meat Cheese*)

1 medium-sized hare
4 ounces ham or bacon, shredded
1 medium sized onion, chopped
1 teaspoon thyme
2 bay leaves
1 teaspoon allspice
1 teaspoon pepper
1 teaspoon salt
1 teaspoon powdered cinnamon
½ cup brandy
¼ cup butter
1 small can pâté de foie gras

Remove meat from bones of hare, dice and mix with ham or bacon. Add onion, seasonings, brandy and butter, and simmer two hours. Remove and grind the mixture so that it forms a paste. Add pâté and press into a mold greased with bacon fat. Stand the mold on a rack in an outer pan of water, cover, and cook very slowly one hour. Cool before turning out of mold. Serve hot, or preferably cold. Yield: six servings.

Chapter 6

Poultry

THE FIRST GESTURE of friendliness and hospitality from the New World to the Old was extended by the cacique or Indian Chief of Tabasco who served the Spaniards a meal of "fowls and fish and other food." Fowl still signifies hospitality in Mexico. Turkey is not a one-day affair or a one-way affair, and although it is preferred in mole sauce, it is served in other delicious dishes. Mexican housewives are skilled in all the forms of preparation. A familiar sight on city streets is the turkey vendor, driving his flock before him and admonishing them gently if they stray while he bargains with a housewife or servant who has answered the whistle.

The Indians also had game of every description—pheasant, quail, pigeons, wild duck and even turtledoves.

Of all fowl, however, chicken is the most popular. Almost everyone who lives in Mexico has a small brood. Even in the city, the custom persists. Roofs and patios of the tenements in the teeming slums of the capital sound and smell also of the barnyard, and in many middle-class neighborhoods the cackle of hens and the crowing of roosters are familiar themes in the morning symphony. Perhaps there are only two or three fowl for eggs today and for the eventual tomorrow when the chicken will turn up in the casserole, disguised in a sauce, or with rice, or fried, or shredded and steaming in tamales, decorating tostadas and rolled in tortillas for tacos and enchiladas.

Chicken is prepared in any number of ways from the practical mancha manteles or tablecloth stainer to the raffish "drunken hen" dish and the more exotic chicken crêpes in salsa verde. Chicken is an everyday affair and is also for fiestas, particularly in small villages when all of the land-owners contribute chickens for the communal fiesta in proportion to their property.

Of almost equal popularity is wild duck.

The eastern coast particularly is a duck hunter's paradise and in many parts of Veracruz, hunting is an occupation. Wild duck is prepared with a rich sauce in the capital city and with subtle spices in the old port of Alvarado, a favorite port of call for Sir John Hawkins and the English buccaneers as well as for the Spanish adventurers. Cold duck served with sherry in that region is a gourmet's delight and even plain duck becomes quite wonderful when cooked in a tradition ten centuries old.

Now and again, sophisticated palates have been regaled with other forms of fowl during Mexican travels. Quail is popular in the north and pheasant has been worked into the Yucatan cuisine, which is a distinct thing and, like the people of the peninsula, demands recognition. Among more exotic fowl are pigeons, which are at their best cooked with the little pine nuts, and turtledoves, a fairly popular dish in knowledgeable Puebla.

POLLO CASERO A LA MEXICANA (*Chicken, Everyday Fashion*)

2½ to 3-pound fryer,
    cut into pieces
3 tablespoons fat
1 onion, chopped fine
1 clove garlic, chopped
2 tomatoes, peeled, chopped
    and drained

1 teaspoon salt
½ teaspoon pepper
2 tablespoons cornstarch
3 large cooked potatoes,
    diced

Fry chicken in fat until golden brown and tender (twenty to thirty minutes). Remove from pan and in the same fat fry the chicken liver. When tender, remove and grind with onion, garlic, tomatoes, salt and pepper. Fry mixture in fat five minutes over low heat. Blend two cups of water with cornstarch, add stirring, to sauce and simmer slowly for twenty minutes. Then add chicken and another cup of water and cook until the chicken is very tender. Add potatoes and simmer four or five minutes longer. Yield: six servings.

FRIJOL CON POLLO (*Beans with Chicken*)

1 cup dried Bayo Gordo or
   Mexican pink beans
1 teaspoon salt
2 tablespoons chopped onion
¼ cup fat

1 tablespoon chili powder
2 cooked chicken breasts,
   diced
½ cup sherry wine

Cook the beans in salted water until tender and drain. Sauté the onion in hot fat. Add chili powder, which has been blended with one tablespoon water, chicken and beans and simmer about ten minutes. Add sherry and simmer for five minutes longer. Yield: six servings.

CREPAS EN SALSA VERDE (*Crêpes with Green Sauce*)

½ cup sifted all-purpose
   flour
½ teaspoon salt

2 eggs, thoroughly beaten
⅔ cup milk
1 tablespoon melted butter

Sift flour and salt. Combine eggs, milk and butter and add to flour. Beat till smooth. For each crêpe, pour about three tablespoons of batter on a hot seven-inch greased griddle. Tilt griddle to spread mixture. When lightly browned, turn and brown on other side. Yield: ten crêpes.

Chicken Filling

1 onion, chopped fine
2 tablespoons fat
2 medium-sized tomatoes,
   peeled and chopped
2 large cooked chicken
   breasts, diced fine

½ cup almonds, blanched
   and sliced
1 tablespoon raisins, chopped
1 tablespoon capers
10 olives, chopped fine

Fry onion in fat until transparent. Add tomatoes and simmer five minutes. Add chicken breasts, almonds, raisins, capers and olives and simmer three minutes. Remove from fire. Place a tablespoon of this mixture in each crêpe, roll and place in a glass baking dish which has been previously buttered. Cover with the following sauce:

Sauce

4 small sweet green peppers	1½ cups milk
2 tablespoons butter	1½ tablespoons cornstarch
2 tablespoons finely chopped onion	½ cup Gruyere cheese, grated

Peel peppers, remove seeds and chop very fine or grind. Heat butter and fry peppers and onion over moderate heat three or four minutes. Add milk in which cornstarch has been blended and simmer slowly about three minutes. Add one-half of the grated cheese and stir until cheese is melted. Pour sauce over the crêpes in the baking dish and sprinkle remaining cheese on top. Bake in a hot oven (425 degrees F.) seven to eight minutes. Yield: five servings.

POLLO A LA POBLANA (*Chicken, Puebla-Style*)

5-pound roaster or fowl, cut up	½ cup fat
	2 chilpotles, canned in vinegar (Page 238)
4 medium-sized tomatoes, peeled and chopped	1 small can sardines, boned
1 large onion, finely chopped	1 teaspoon salt
4 cloves garlic, chopped	1 teaspoon pepper
3 sprigs parsley, chopped	1 medium-sized head lettuce

Clean chicken thoroughly. Cook in sufficient water to cover; one hour for a roaster or three hours for a fowl. Fry tomatoes, onion, garlic and parsley in the fat about ten minutes. Add one cup of chicken stock and simmer ten minutes. Add chilpotles, cut in strips, chicken and sardines. Cook slowly until the liquid has almost evaporated. Season with salt and pepper. Serve garnished with lettuce leaves. Yield: six servings.

POLLO ADOBADO (*Spiced Chicken*)

4-pound fowl or roaster
1 medium-sized onion, chopped
5 cloves garlic, chopped
3 sprigs parsley, chopped
½ cup vinegar
½ cup water
1 teaspoon salt
2 laurel leaves
¼ cup flour
½ cup fat

Clean fowl, leave whole or cut into serving pieces. Half cover with boiling water and simmer fowl three to four hours; roaster one to one and a-half hours, or until tender. Add water if needed. Cool for several hours or if possible overnight. Bone chicken and put in a pan with onion, garlic, parsley, vinegar and water, salt and laurel leaves. Allow the chicken to stand in the mixture three hours, stirring occasionally with a wooden spoon. Remove chicken, drain, dip in flour and fry in fat until a golden brown. Yield: five or six servings.

MOLE SENCILLO (*Simple Mole*)

4 to 5-pound drawn roaster or fowl, cut up
3 chilies pasilla (Page 238)
3 chilies anchos (Page 238)
½ cup peanuts, peeled and ground
¼ teaspoon cloves
1 teaspoon powdered cinnamon
½ teaspoon pepper
2 cloves garlic, chopped
1 tablespoon salt
¼ cup fat

Half cover the fowl with boiling water. Simmer fowl covered for three to four hours; roaster one to one and a-half hours. Add a little more water if needed. Grind chilies and mix with peanuts, cloves, cinnamon, pepper, garlic and salt and fry in the fat for about five minutes. Add one and a half cups of the chicken stock slowly, stirring constantly. Then add the chicken pieces and simmer slowly for twenty to thirty minutes. It may be necessary to add a little more stock, although the sauce should be quite thick. Yield: four to five servings.

FIAMBRE (*Cold Lunch*)

1 young chicken (*about 3 pounds*)
1 small calf's tongue
2 fresh pig's feet
1 small head lettuce, shredded
3 medium-sized tomatoes, peeled and sliced
1 large onion, sliced very thin
½ cup olive oil
¼ cup vinegar
1 teaspoon salt
½ teaspoon pepper
1 orange, peeled and sliced
3 avocados, sliced
1 small bunch radishes

Cook the chicken, tongue and pig's feet in water until so tender that the meat separates easily from the bones. Remove meat, cool and dice. Marinate lettuce, tomatoes and onion with a dressing made of the oil, vinegar, salt and pepper. Add the diced meats and toss together. Garnish with orange, avocados and radishes. Yield: eight servings.

GALLINA TABASQUEÑA (*Hen, Tabasco-Style*)

4½- to 5-pound roasting chicken or fowl, cut up
Juice of one lime or sour orange
1 tablespoon salt
4 tablespoons fat
4 medium-sized onions, finely chopped
6 medium-sized tomatoes, peeled, chopped and drained
2 tablespoons chopped olives
1 tablespoon capers
2 tablespoons seedless raisins
2 tablespoons seeded prunes, chopped
¼ pound ham, finely chopped
½ cup almonds, blanched
8 cloves garlic, diced
2 tablespoons vinegar
2 tablespoons olive oil
½ teaspoon pepper
4 cloves
½ teaspoon pepper
2-inch stick cinnamon
3 canned pimientos, shredded

Rub chicken with lime or orange juice and sprinkle with salt. Fry until golden brown in fat. Add all other ingredients except pimientos and fry about ten minutes. Add one and a half cups water. Cover and simmer until hen is tender, one hour or longer. Serve with thickened sauce and garnish with pimiento strips. Yield: six servings.

GALLINAS BORRACHAS (*Drunken Hens*)

3-pound fryer, cut up	*¼ cup sugar*
½ cup shortening	*¼ teaspoon cloves*
2 large tomatoes, peeled, chopped, drained	*¼ teaspoon cinnamon*
	¼ teaspoon pepper
1 teaspoon parsley, chopped	*⅛ teaspoon nutmeg*
	½ cup seedless raisins
1 medium-sized onion, chopped	*¼ cup blanched almonds, chopped*
½ pound ham, chopped	*2 tablespoons bread crumbs*
1 Mexican sausage, chopped	
2 cups dry sherry wine	

Fry chicken in shortening, reserving one tablespoon. Add tomatoes, parsley, and onion, and fry about eight minutes. Add ham, sausage, sherry, sugar, spice, raisins and almonds. Cover and simmer twenty minutes. Just before removing from heat fry breadcrumbs in remaining tablespoon of shortening and add to chicken. Yield: four servings.

POLLO A LA MEXICANA (*Chicken, Mexican-Style*)

4- to 5-pound drawn fowl or roaster	*1 medium-sized onion, chopped*
2 tablespoons fat	*2 tablespoons peanut butter*
3 large tomatoes, peeled and chopped	*¼ cup dry sherry wine*
	½ cup light cream

Half cover chicken with boiling water and simmer, covered, one hour. Remove. Cut chicken into portions and fry in fat till browned. Add tomatoes, onion and one cup of chicken stock and simmer, covered, one hour or until tender. Add peanut butter which has been mixed with half-cup of stock and simmer ten minutes. Add wine, bring to a boil and add the cream. Yield: five or six servings.

POLLO CON SALSA DE PIÑONES (*Chicken with Pine Nut Sauce*)

2- to 3-pound frying chicken	2 tablespoons sugar
½ cup pine nuts, blanched	2 tablespoons flour
½ cup shortening	2 tablespoons butter
½ cup sherry wine	¼ cup raisins
1 tablespoon cinnamon	¼ cup almonds

Quarter chicken and stew till tender in a small amount of salted water. Grind pine nuts and brown lightly in shortening. Add sherry, cinnamon, chicken, one cup chicken stock and sugar. Brown flour in butter, add to chicken and simmer fifteen minutes. Add raisins and almonds. Yield: four servings.

POLLO CON ARROZ (*Chicken with Rice*)

1 cup rice	Salt and cumin seed to taste
1 frying chicken	Fat for frying
½ clove garlic	2 tomatoes, chopped
½ onion	2 small green peppers,
4 black peppers	sliced

Soak rice in warm water fifteen minutes and drain. Cut chicken in pieces. Grind together garlic, onion, black peppers, salt and cumin seed and spread over the raw pieces of chicken. Fry chicken in very hot fat until partly browned and add rice.

Cook until rice begins to brown, add tomatoes and fry five minutes. Add a quart of cold water, another pinch of salt and the green peppers. Cover and cook slowly until the rice is soft. Before removing from fire, grind and add cooked chicken liver. Yield: five servings.

POLLOS TAPATIOS (*Chicken, Jalisco-Style*)

2 spring chickens
½ pound ham
½ pound pork loin
1 onion
2 cloves garlic
2 laurel leaves
1 teaspoon marjoram
1 teaspoon salt

¼ cup vinegar
3 cups water
4 strips bacon, chopped
½ pound tiny potatoes, boiled
2 Mexican sausages, diced
4 chilpotles, canned (Page 238)

Simmer together covered for one hour and twenty minutes chicken, ham, pork, onion, garlic, laurel, marjoram, salt, vinegar and water. Cut chicken into small portions, shred ham and pork. In two cups of the broth boil, covered, thirty minutes, bacon, potatoes, sausages, chilpotles, chicken, ham and pork. Yield: six servings.

PASTEL DE POLLO (*Chicken Pie*)

2 fryers (about 3 pounds)
1 onion, quartered
2 cloves garlic
1 tablespoon vinegar
½ pound ham
1 teaspoon salt
1 cup water
1 pinch pepper
½ teaspoon nutmeg
½ cup butter

1 cup cream
1 sprig parsley, chopped
1 can or ½ cup mushrooms
1 small can truffles, sliced
2 green peppers, chopped
2 carrots, thinly sliced
½ cup diced, cooked celery
2 eggs, beaten lightly
2 hard-cooked eggs

Simmer together, covered, one and one-half to three hours, or until chicken is tender, chicken, onion, garlic, vinegar, ham, salt and water. Drain. Chop ham and chicken meat. Add pepper, nutmeg, butter, cream, parsley, mushrooms, truffles and juice, peppers, carrots, celery and beaten eggs. Pour half of the mixture into a greased casserole and cover with sliced hard-cooked eggs. Add rest of chicken mixture. Set casserole in a pan of water and bake in a slow oven (325 degrees F.) thirty minutes. Cool slightly. Garnish with additional slices of peppers and sprigs of parsley. Yield: six to eight servings.

MANCHA MANTELES (*Tablecloth Stainers*)

1 4- to 5-pound roaster or drawn fowl
½ pound lean pork meat
¼ cup shortening
2 red peppers
¾ cup blanched almonds
2 teaspoons sesame seeds
½ pound tomatoes, peeled and chopped
1 teaspoon salt
1 slice fresh or canned pineapple, diced
1 apple, peeled, cored and diced
¼ cup sugar
1 sliced banana
1 medium-sized sweet potato, cooked, diced
1 slice jicama or ½ apple
1 teaspoon powdered cinnamon

Cut chicken into portions. Fry pork until brown and then simmer in a small amount of water, covered, thirty minutes. Fry the pieces of chicken in shortening until golden brown. Remove. In the same pan fry peppers, almonds and sesame seeds. Remove and grind together. Add tomatoes and press mixture through a colander. Add to chicken. Add pork, salt, and remaining ingredients. Cover and simmer one hour. Yield: six servings.

PATO (*Duck*)

4 to 5-pound dressed duck
4 tablespoons lemon juice
¼ cup vinegar
1 teaspoon salt
1 teaspoon pepper
4 onion tops, cut into
  pieces
3 cups water

4 large tomatoes, peeled
  and chopped
2 medium-sized onions,
  chopped
2 cloves garlic, chopped
¼ cup olive oil
15 olives
1 tablespoon capers

Draw duck, singe if necessary and cut off neck close to the body. Remove any pinfeathers, wash thoroughly inside and out. Rub duck well with lemon juice, rinse with cold water and cut into good-sized portions. Cook with vinegar, salt, pepper, onion tops and water for one hour.

Fry tomatoes, onion, garlic and pepper and salt to taste in olive oil three or four minutes. Pour half of the fried sauce into a pot, cover with pieces of duck and add the remaining sauce. Cook over very low heat until the sauce is dry and the duck is brown. Garnish with olives and capers. Yield: four servings.

PATO ALVARADEÑO (*Duck, Alvarado-Style*)

4-pound duck
1 teaspoon salt
¼ cup fat
1 medium-sized onion
2 slices ham, shredded
1 slice bacon, shredded

½ teaspoon salt
½ teaspoon pepper
1 tablespoon bread crumbs
2 sprigs parsley, chopped
  fine

Clean duck thoroughly and cut into serving portions. Simmer until tender and strain. Sprinkle with salt and fry in fat over slow heat for thirty minutes, turning to brown all sides. Add onion, ham, bacon, salt and pepper. Cover and cook ten minutes. Remove cover, add bread crumbs, one-fourth cup water and parsley and simmer another ten minutes. Serve very hot. Yield: four servings.

PATO A LA CAMPECHANA (*Duck, Campeche-Style*)

1 teaspoon salt	2 cloves garlic
1 teaspoon pepper	1 cup dry sherry wine
¼ cup vinegar	2 tablespoons flour
2 two-pound wild ducks	1 large tomato, peeled,
½ cup fat	chopped, drained
1 teaspoon cinnamon	1 large onion, chopped
2 cloves	4 sprigs parsley, chopped
⅛ teaspoon saffron	2 cups canned peas, strained

Mix salt, pepper and vinegar. Let stand ten minutes. With a sharp knife remove meat of ducks from bones and moisten it well with salted vinegar. Fry ducks in half the fat. Mix cinnamon, cloves, saffron and garlic with the sherry and add duck. Brown flour in the rest of fat. Add tomato, onion and parsley and fry five minutes. Add to ducks and simmer over a low flame thirty minutes or until meat is tender, adding one cup of stock or hot water if needed. About two minutes before removing from the fire, add pea purée. Yield: four servings.

PATO A LA VERACRUZANA (*Duck, Veracruz-Style*)

4 to five-pound duck	2 cloves garlic, chopped fine
1 tablespoon salt	¼ teaspoon cumin
1 cup almonds, blanched	1 egg yolk, well beaten
and ground	2 tablespoons fat

Clean duck thoroughly inside and out and cut into serving portions. Cover with about three cups of water, add salt and cook until tender. Mix almonds, garlic and cumin with egg yolk and fry the mixture in the fat for three minutes. Add one and a-half cups of duck stock and duck and simmer slowly until the sauce thickens. Yield: four servings.

MOLE DE GUAJOLOTE (*Turkey in Mole Sauce*)

4 *chilies anchos* (Page 238) 2-*inch stick cinnamon*
4 *chilies mulatos* (Page 238) 5 *peppercorns*
4 *chilies pasillas* (Page 238) 2 *cloves*
1 *onion, roasted* ½ *teaspoon aniseed*
2 *tablespoons sesame seeds* 1 *teaspoon salt*
2 *tablespoons shelled* ½ *tortilla, fried*
   peanuts 4 *tablespoons fat*
1 *square* (*one ounce*) 3 *pounds turkey, fresh*
   cooking chocolate   *or frozen parts*

To make mole sauce soak chilies, remove veins, and grind onion with chilies. Heat together sesame, peanuts, chocolate, spices, salt and the fried tortilla. Grind together. Fry all the ingredients in hot fat about three minutes. Add half cup of water and continue to cook over low heat until the sauce is thick and well blended. (Preparation of this dish has been simplified during recent years by the advent of some excellent canned and powered mole sauces that are sold in most Mexican food stores. These sauces have become very popular even in Mexico where the cheapness of household help makes labor-saving devices of little consequence.)

Cut turkey into serving pieces and stew gently in enough water to cover till tender. Drain, cover with mole sauce and simmer, covered, seven or eight minutes. If the sauce is too thick, add a little turkey broth. Yield: six servings.

MOLE SERRANO (*Mountain Mole*)

10- *to 12-pound turkey* ⅓ *cup cracker crumbs*
3 *chilies anchos* (Page 238) 20 *cloves*
3 *large tomatoes, peeled and* 2 *two-inch sticks cinnamon*
   chopped 1 *cup fat*
½ *pound blanched almonds* 2 *tablespoons salt*
3 *ounces seedless raisins* 1 *teaspoon sugar*
1 *banana* ¼ *cup toasted sesame seeds*
3 *squares chocolate* *Grated cheese*

Clean turkey, cut into portions and cook in enough water to cover until tender. Remove seeds from chilies, toast lightly over direct flame and soak in two cups of water for one hour. Chop together the chilies, tomatoes, almonds, raisins, banana, chocolate, cracker crumbs, cloves and cinnamon. Fry in the fat about ten minutes. Add salt and simmer another five minutes. Add the stock in which the turkey was cooked, pouring it in slowly and stirring constantly. Add sugar and cook slowly until the sauce is very thick. Put cooked turkey pieces in the pot with other ingredients and simmer a few minutes. Remove. Serve sprinkled with sesame. Yield: ten to twelve servings.

TORTOLAS POBLANAS (*Turtledoves, Puebla-Style*)

10 turtledoves
1 teaspoon salt
4 tablespoons butter
2 tablespoons flour
1 cup white wine
1 cup stock
4 sprigs parsley, chopped
2 canned chilies, cut into strips
2 cloves garlic
4 tortillas (bought), cut into triangles
2 tablespoons fat

Clean the turtledoves, sprinkle with salt and fry in the butter until golden. Without removing them from the pan, sprinkle with flour. Then add the wine, stock, parsley, chilies and garlic and simmer about ten minutes. Serve covered with sauce and garnish with tortillas which have been fried in fat to a golden brown. Yield: five servings.

Chapter 7

Other Main Dishes—
Beans, Eggs and Cheese

SOMEHOW, somewhere, lost in the mist of antiquity and legend, the peoples of Mexico found beans.

Although there is uncertainty about where they originated, beans are known to have been used throughout Central, North and South America. The Mohicans and the tribes of the northeast United States ate the huge Lima beans which came from Peru. And everywhere on the continent, people ate white beans and black beans, pea beans, black-eyed beans, kidney beans, flat shell beans and even string beans. They do still and the ways in which ancient people prepared them are still favorite ways of cooking.

The Spaniards had never seen beans before they arrived. As a matter of fact, no one in Europe had, for the only types of beans not indigenous to the New World are the soy beans of the Far East and the broad beans of Europe, which are not really beans at all. Beans probably did more than anything else to encourage the settlement of the New World and trade between the Old World and this continent, for with beans the sailors had means of sustenance on long voyages. As in the United States, beans were not and have never been a matter of class distinction.

The appropriation of beans by the Massachusetts settlers was a repetition of what had occurred a century earlier in Mexico where they became an inevitable part of any creole meal. For centuries, beans provided the Indian peoples with most of their protein. For the past 400 years, they have provided Mexico with its most familiar food. No meal is complete without frijoles.

Beans in one form or another are eaten at any time. The huge Lima beans, toasted and dusted with chili powder, have become favorite cocktail snacks. So are chick peas prepared in the same way. Beans are used to make candy and dessert.

Beans are made into soups and into a thick purée to spread in tacos, enchiladas, tortas and tostadas.

Of the fabulous variety, the most common is the Bayo Gordo, for which pinto or pink beans may be substituted in the United States. The most common way of preparing them is in Frijoles de Olla or boiled in a clay pot for a long time and served in the thick broth. A dish of beans from the pot and a few tortillas are the staple of the Indian diet and a simple solution to the problem of what to have for breakfast, dinner and supper. Even in fashionable restaurants and in homes in the city, Frijoles de Olla are popular.

Another favorite is Frijoles Refritos. For this dish the Frijoles de Olla are drained, mashed and fried. A simple way to prepare Frijoles Refritos in the United States is to buy canned beans of the thicker variety, already cooked, and fry them according to the Mexican recipe. Fried beans are served quite simply just before the dessert course or they appear more elaborately as the roll of beans adorned with avocados, radishes and grated cheese. A delicious way to serve them is in the form of mitos, small rolls of fried beans filled with sardines, floured, dipped in beaten egg, fried and served with onion and tomato sauce.

In any part of Mexico, the clay olla of beans bubbling on the charcoal fire and the waiting pottery dish is hospitality.

FRIJOLES CON PLATANOS (*Beans and Bananas*)

3 very ripe frying bananas	⅔ cup cooked or canned
3 tablespoons flour	beans
4 tablespoons melted butter	⅔ cup shortening

Mash bananas, add flour and butter and mix thoroughly. Fry the beans in one tablespoon shortening for about five minutes. Heat remaining shortening in another frying pan, add banana mixture, one tablespoon at a time, and spread with a fork so that it will take the shape of a small pancake. Fry the "pancakes" for about five minutes, place a teaspoon of the fried beans on each and fold. Fry the stuffed pancakes, covered, three minutes on each side or until brown. Yield: six servings.

CORONA DE FRIJOL (*Crown of Beans*)

1 cup small red beans, cooked	3 tablespoons melted butter
6 ounces American cheese	1 teaspoon salt
1 medium-sized onion, chopped	¼ cup bread crumbs
2 eggs, well beaten	2 Mexican sausages, chopped, fried

Fry beans as in Mexican Beans (See following recipe). Grind together beans and cheese. Add onion, eggs, two tablespoons melted butter and salt and mix well.

Grease a ring mold and sprinkle it with bread crumbs. Pour in the bean mixture and press it down well. Cover with bread crumbs and the remaining butter in small chunks. Bake in a moderate oven (350 degrees F.) about ten minutes. Serve very hot, garnished with sausages. Yield: six servings.

FRIJOLES MEXICANOS (*Mexican Refried Beans*)

4 tablespoons lard	½ cup tomato purée
1 tablespoon chopped onion	2 cups frijoles (Mexican beans)

Soak beans overnight and cook, covered, in five cups of water one and a half to two hours, or until very tender. Drain. Heat two tablespoons lard in a frying pan, add beans and fry over low heat about ten minutes, mashing them with a fork. Add water in which beans were cooked a little at a time, stirring constantly, and keep over a low flame until the water has evaporated. Cool and place in a refrigerator until the following day.

Fry onion a few minutes in two tablespoons lard, add tomato purée and chili pepper if desired. When onion is tender, add fried beans and cook until beans are very hot. Yield: six servings.

FRIJOLES DE OLLA (*Pot Beans*)

2 cups frijoles (*Mexican*   ⅓ pound salt pork
    beans)

Soak beans overnight. Drain and cover with fresh cold
water. Add salt pork and boil slowly until tender, four to six
hours. As water boils away, replace it with boiling water.
Yield: ten servings.

EGGS

Eggs, like many other foods in Mexico, are a matter of
quality not quantity.

The approved method of buying and selling is one or two
or three or four at a time or in huge baskets. It depends on
the size of the family, the size of the purse, refrigeration, or
whether or not one has made some very informal contract
with a campesino who will come from Guanajuato, Jalisco,
Puebla or some other nearby state on more or less specified
days of the month with eggs, fruit and meat for sale.

In stores, even in the great new shining super-mercados
with their rows of canned foods from all parts of the globe,
eggs are sold individually, not in dozen lots. In the rare times
when prices rise, there is always a cluster of angry housewives
around the huge basket, where they keep gesticulating vio-
lently and making musical protest.

Eggs have always been considered something of a delicacy
in Mexico. Not infrequently you will see them beside other
donations at the great basilica of Guadalupe. An egg is properly considered a gift by the most impoverished of the pilgrims come to pay tribute.

Another indication that eggs are a sign of plenty is the
luxuriousness of the manner in which they are served. Few
Mexicans with a respect for the national cuisine would dream
of eating a soft boiled egg or a poached egg. Eggs were meant

to adorn and to be adorned. In huge quantities they go into rich desserts. The sweet Huevos Reales is nothing more than a sponge made of egg yolks, baked, and preserved in thick syrup. Eggs belong with chocolate to enrich it even further and to be whirled into a sweet froth. Eggs and vegetables are a natural marriage and together they produce the delicious soufflés and puddings which give character even to such humble things as turnips. Eggs go uncooked into the rich flavor of garlic broth and are boiled in the fragrant steam at the table.

Eggs are a vehicle for unparalleled triumphs with sauces as they are prepared in Puebla or by the delicious southern method with a chartreuse-colored sauce, or in the northern spicy manner. Some wonderful ways to use them are as accompaniments with avocado, beans, bananas and with fried rice. The final compliment is to prepare them with wine or with Mexican brandy.

For breakfast, eggs are eaten scrambled and piquant with tiny slices of chili and pimiento beaten through them. Even more delicious, however, is the dish called Huevos Rancheros. In this fried eggs are served on a bed of tortilla and covered with a rich awakening sauce.

HUEVOS CON SALSA DE AGUACATES (*Eggs with Avocado Sauce*)

¼ cup cream
1 tablespoon cornstarch
1 teaspoon salt
½ teaspoon pepper

3 large avocados, peeled and mashed
12 hot, hard-cooked eggs

Mix cream with cornstarch, salt and pepper and cook, stirring, till thickened, about five minutes. Add the avocados which have been passed through a sieve. Cut eggs in half and serve covered with avocado sauce. Yield: six servings.

HUEVOS A LA CREMA (*Creamed Eggs*)

2 tablespoons fat	¼ cup bread crumbs
1 medium-sized onion, chopped	¼ cup grated cheese
	2 tablespoons butter
2 large tomatoes, peeled, drained	1 egg yolk, beaten
	¼ cup cream
1 teaspoon salt	6 hard-cooked eggs
½ teaspoon pepper	

Fry together in fat, onion, tomatoes, salt and pepper for five minutes. Add bread crumbs, cheese, butter, egg yolk and cream and simmer, covered, for fifteen minutes. Cut hard-cooked eggs in half lengthwise and cover with the sauce. Yield: four servings.

HUEVOS CON CREMA (*Eggs with Cream*)

10 eggs	2 tablespoons butter
1 teaspoon salt	2 teaspoons cinnamon
1 cup heavy cream	

Beat the eggs lightly with salt and add the cream. Melt the butter in a large frying pan and pour in the egg mixture. Cook as an omelet. When almost done sprinkle with cinnamon. Yield: six servings.

HUEVOS ESTRELLADOS (*Fried Eggs*)

6 eggs	2 tablespoons butter
2 tablespoons fat	½ tablespoon olive oil
2 teaspoons salt	1 teaspoon vinegar
3 medium-sized tomatoes, chopped, drained	2 canned green pickled peppers
1 onion, chopped	4 oz. cream cheese
1 teaspoon cilantro (or use chopped parsley)	

Fry eggs one at a time in fat. Place each on a hot platter and sprinkle with salt. Cover the eggs with sauce made by frying tomatoes, onion and cilantro or parsley in butter three minutes. Add olive oil and vinegar. Garnish with slices of peppers and cheese. Yield: three servings.

HUEVOS CON PLATANO (*Eggs with Banana*)

3 eggs, separated
2 bananas, sliced
1 tablespoon butter
½ teaspoon salt
1 tablespoon olive oil

Beat egg whites, then yolks and fold together. Add the bananas, butter and salt and fry in oil about three minutes. Yield: two or three servings.

HUEVOS CON MACARRÓN (*Eggs with Macaroni*)

1 cup elbow macaroni
1 cup tomato purée
2 teaspoons salt
1 teaspoon pepper
2 tablespoons fat
6 eggs
3 tablespoons butter

Cook the macaroni in one and one-half quarts boiling water until tender. Drain and rinse in cold water. Mix tomato purée, salt and pepper and fry in the fat three minutes. Mix macaroni and sauce and turn into a greased glass baking dish. Make six depressions in the surface. Bake in a moderate oven (375 degrees F.) ten minutes. Remove and break a raw egg into each depression. Dot the entire surface with little chunks of butter. Return to oven and bake five minutes or until eggs are cooked. Yield: six servings.

RABO DE MESTIZA (*Eggs, Mestiza-Style*)

3 *sweet peppers*
1 *tablespoon butter*
1 *onion, chopped*
1 *tablespoon chopped parsley*
1 *cup canned tomatoes*

1 *cup milk, scalded*
1 *cup cream*
3 *ounces cream cheese, chopped*
6 *hard-cooked eggs, sliced*

Peel sweet peppers, remove seeds and cut into strips. Fry in butter with onion, parsley and tomatoes about ten minutes. Add milk, cream and cheese and simmer over very low heat about eight minutes. Before serving, add eggs. Yield: four to six servings.

TORTILLA MEXICANA (*Mexican Omelet*)

6 *eggs*
½ *teaspoon salt*
20 *olives, chopped*
1 *tablespoon capers*

2 *small green canned chilies, chopped fine*
1 *tablespoon butter*

Beat eggs well with salt. Add olives, capers and chilies and fry slowly in butter. Yield: three to four servings.

HUEVOS PIRIPI (*Eggs Piripi*)

½ *cup butter*
1 *tablespoon flour*
½ *cup walnuts or pecans, ground*
1 *cup milk*

1 *teaspoon salt*
½ *teaspoon pepper*
¼ *teaspoon nutmeg*
6 *hard-cooked eggs, sliced*
½ *cup bread crumbs*

Melt one-quarter cup butter, blend in flour and cook, stirring, about three minutes. Add nuts, milk, salt, pepper and nutmeg and simmer five minutes. In a buttered baking dish arrange layers of egg slices, sauce, bread crumbs and tiny chunks of remaining butter. Bake in a moderate oven (325 degrees F.) about eight minutes. Yield: four servings.

HUEVOS POTOSI (*Eggs, Potosi-Style*)

6 hard-cooked eggs
½ cup grated cheese
1¼ cups boiled chopped
    spinach
3 tablespoons butter

1 tablespoon cream
Salt and pepper to taste
½ teaspoon nutmeg
1¼ cups medium white
    sauce

Cut eggs in half lengthwise, remove yolks and mash with half the grated cheese. Fill whites with mixture. Mix spinach with one tablespoon butter, cream, salt, pepper and nutmeg. Put mixture in a buttered baking dish, add stuffed eggs and cover with white sauce. Sprinkle with remaining cheese and dot with the rest of butter. Bake in a slow oven (325 degrees F.) ten or twelve minutes. Yield: four servings.

HUEVOS RANCHEROS (*Ranchero Eggs*)

1 onion, chopped
3 small green peppers,
    chopped
6 tablespoons tomato sauce
6 tablespoons grated cheese

Salt and pepper
6 thin tortillas
6 eggs
Avocado slices or fried
    sausage

Mix together onion, peppers, tomato sauce, cheese, salt and pepper. Fry tortillas till light brown in deep fat and place a fried egg on each. Cover with the uncooked sauce, garnish with avocado slices or fried sausage and serve hot. Yield: six servings.

HUEVOS REVUELTOS (*Scrambled Eggs*)

1 teaspoon chopped onion	1 tomato, peeled and chopped
3 tablespoons fat	1 teaspoon chili powder
1 teaspoon chopped parsley	6 eggs, well beaten

Fry onion in fat until golden. Add parsley, tomato and chili powder and fry two or three minutes longer. Add eggs and cook over moderate heat, stirring constantly, until done. Serve on toast or Mexican Rice (Page 55). Yield: four servings.

TAMALES DE HUEVO (*Egg Tamales*)

1 pound nixtamalina (packaged or canned), or	12 egg yolks
1 pound white corn meal	2 tablespoons sugar
1½ cups butter, melted	Corn leaves
1¼ cups fat, melted	¼ cup seedless raisins
	¼ cup blanched almonds

Mix the nixtamalina or corn meal with the cooled butter and fat. Beat egg yolks with one-half cup water and sugar, add to nixtamalina and let stand half-an-hour. Beat thoroughly for about thirty minutes or until a spoonful of the dough when dropped in a cup of cold water will rise in a unified manner to the top. Make the tamales according to the recipe for Tamales de Picadillo (Page 71) or Tamales de Almendra (Page 68), placing some of the mixture on the corn leaves in the same way and filling them with a mixture of raisins and almonds, chopped fine. Yield: two to two and one-half dozen.

HUEVOS EN SALSA DE VINO (*Eggs with Wine Sauce*)

1 tablespoon butter	½ teaspoon pepper
1 tablespoon flour	1 teaspoon French mustard
½ cup hot water	2 tablespoons lemon juice
½ cup white wine	6 hot hard-cooked eggs
1 teaspoon salt	

Melt butter, blend in flour, add water and cook, stirring until the mixture is thick. Boil two minutes longer. Add wine, salt, pepper, mustard and the lemon juice in drops, while stirring. Simmer a minute or two longer.

Halve eggs, cover with hot sauce and serve immediately. Yield: four servings.

QUESO RELLENO (*Stuffed Cheese with Sauce*)

1 Edam or other Holland-type cheese	20 blanched almonds, halved
2 tablespoons shortening	18 olives, halved
½ pound pork loin ground	1 sweet pepper, peeled and chopped
1 small onion, chopped	
2 teaspoons tomato purée	1 teaspoon vinegar
1 tablespoon salt	3 hard-cooked eggs
Pepper	

Cut a square from the top of the cheese sufficiently large so that the center of the cheese may be scooped out with a spoon, leaving a hollow wall about half an inch thick. Scrape away the red outer covering of cheese.

Brown in shortening half the pork and the onion. Add tomato purée, salt and pepper, almonds, olives, sweet pepper and vinegar. Place the hard-cooked eggs inside the hollowed cheese and press them down with the meat mixture. Cover with the square of cheese and seal with a thick paste made of flour and water. Wrap the stuffed cheese in a piece of greased parchment and cook in a covered double boiler about fifteen minutes or until it is soft. Serve covered with the following sauce:

Sauce

2 tablespoons flour	1 teaspoon salt
2 cups water	⅛ teaspoon pepper
2 tablespoons butter	1 small onion, chopped

Blend flour with a small amount of water. Heat remaining water, add flour and mix, stirring, add remaining ingredients and cook, stirring, until thickened. Yield: six servings.

Chapter 8

Vegetables and Salads

As FAR BACK as there is any knowledge, corn was the all-important gift of the soil. Even beyond knowledge, it was an intimate part of religious myths and rites. Temples rose everywhere in the land to honor Centeotl the Goddess of Earth and Maize. Three festivals a year were held in her honor. Each spring when the ancient Aztecs performed rites to venerate the God of the Peaked Volcano, Popocatepetl, priests covered crooked branches with a paste made of amaranth seeds and corn. When the Aztec heroes rejoined their ancestors, it was with thin cakes of corn beside them and honey and jewels to pay their way.

In Mexico today, corn, ground on the metates, which were used long before the Conquest, and in the form of tortillas, is still the pièce de résistance of every meal, but the ever-present tortillas are only part of the corn saga. Corn meal steamed in husks or banana leaves with meat and chili or sprinkled with raisins and candied fruits are the morning and evening tamales. Tortillas are wrapped around beans, cheese or the flowers of squash to create tacos, and with a thick sauce become enchiladas. The atoles are made of ground corn and water sweetened with sugar or honey. Pozole is taken on journeys and to the fields by the peasants. Pinole is a refreshing beverage made of ground popped corn. On any corner in any city you may buy ears of corn freshly roasted.

Corn was the great gift.

And aside from corn flakes and a few other corn foods of current manufacture, the people of Mexico and of the world are still eating corn foods in the same form they were known to the Indians thousands of years ago: popped corn, roasting corn, sweet corn, hominy and grits, hulled corn, corn pudding, corn meal mush, corn bread.

Corn is all important, but other vegetables are an essential part of the national diet, too.

The discovery of America was of tremendous importance to Europe. Among other things, it meant that the diet of the people of the Old World was doubled. Europe owes melons to the New World, beans, corn, tomatoes, peppers, avocados, and a host of different root vegetables, including the potato. Despite the fact that potatoes come from this hemisphere, they are not popular in Mexico, except the sweet potato, the oldest of all American root crops. In Mexico they are called by a more indigenous name—camotes. Camotes are used to make candy, dessert, cakes, and are also served as a vegetable with the meal.

Mexicans are not fond of plain boiled vegetables and they have conceived hundreds of cunning ways to disguise and adorn them. Vegetables come in soufflé, stuffed, cooked with elaborate sauces, creamed, and they are used to stuff pastry and in delectable casseroles.

There was no type of squash not developed by the Indians, but most popular in Mexico is the small green squash, called zucchini in the United States. This is served hot and cold, stuffed and rather simply, but the favorite way is in a creamy nut sauce brightened with pomegranate seeds.

The gay orange flowers of the squash are another favorite vegetable and make a particularly delicious dish.

Chayotes or christophine, the light green rough fruit of a climbing vine, is also a favorite vegetable. It is cooked like squash and is served sliced, mashed, with sauce, breaded and fried or made into a delicious vegetable pudding. Among other popular "greens" are romeritos, cooked with shrimp patties for Lent, and nopales, the tender pulpy leaves of the cactus. These are combined with eggs for a savory and satisfying Lenten dish.

Very popular are the sweet large chilies which are used in salads, sauces and as vegetables. The Puebla Chilies en Nogada are the traditional dish on the day of Saint Augustine each August.

ALCACHOFAS REINA (*Queen Artichokes*)

6 artichokes	2 tablespoons olive oil
1 lime, halved	2 large tomatoes, peeled and
Salt and pepper	drained
1 tablespoon flour	2 tablespoons grated cheese
1 small onion, chopped fine	½ cup sweet cream
1 sweet pepper, chopped	1 tablespoon bread crumbs

Remove outer leaves of the artichokes, simmer hearts, covered, thirty minutes in two quarts of water with lime, salt, pepper and flour which has been blended with a little water. When tender, transfer to a baking dish. Fry onion and sweet pepper in oil until lightly browned. Add chopped tomatoes, fry two or three minutes longer. Add cheese and salt, remove from fire and add cream. Cover artichokes with sauce, sprinkle with crumbs and bake in a moderate oven (350 degrees F.) about ten minutes. Serve very hot. Yield: six servings.

AGUACATES RELLENOS (*Stuffed Avocados*)

1 pound chopped beef	20 blanched almonds
⅛ teaspoon salt	10 olives, pitted
1 clove garlic	¼ cup seedless raisins
¾ cup shortening	2 small pickled peppers
2 medium-sized onions,	6 avocados
chopped	2 tablespoons flour
1¼ cup tomato purée	3 eggs, beaten
⅛ teaspoon pepper	1 head lettuce
Pinch cumin seed	6 radishes

Simmer meat in water to cover with salt and garlic thirty minutes. Heat two tablespoons of shortening and fry one-quarter of the onions, one-quarter cup of tomato purée, the pepper, cumin, almonds, olives, raisins and pickled peppers about ten minutes or until the moisture has been absorbed. Add meat. Peel avocados, cut in half lengthwise, remove seed and stuff with the meat mixture. Fit two halves together and pin with picks. Sprinkle avocados with flour and dip into the eggs. Fry in remaining shortening. Place avocados in a casserole. Fry the remaining tomato purée in one tablespoon shortening and add the rest of the chopped onion. Simmer over low heat for five minutes. Pour over avocados and bake in a slow oven (325 degrees F.) five minutes or until heated thoroughly. Yield: six servings.

COLIFLOR ESTILO PUEBLA (*Puebla-Style Cauliflower*)

1 medium cauliflower	2 cloves
3 tomatoes, chopped	1 stick cinnamon
½ sweet red pepper, chopped	Salt and pepper
	2 bay leaves
4 tablespoons olive oil	1 tablespoon capers
1 onion, chopped	1 tablespoon chopped olives
1 clove garlic, chopped	
4 teaspoons chopped parsley	3 tablespoons fine bread crumbs
1 small chili Jalapeño (Page 238)	2 tablespoons grated cheese

Cook cauliflower in salted water until tender and drain. Fry one tomato with red pepper in three tablespoons oil for three or four minutes. Add the remainder of tomatoes, onion, garlic, parsley and chili and simmer slowly for ten minutes. Add cloves, cinnamon, salt, pepper and bay leaves and cook a few minutes. Before removing from stove, add capers and olives. Cool. Pour some of the sauce in a greased baking dish, add cauliflower which has been separated into flowerets and cover with remaining sauce. Add bread crumbs, grated cheese and one tablespoon of oil. Bake in a hot oven (400 degrees F.) eight to ten minutes. Serve very hot. Yield: six servings.

CHAYOTES EMPANIZADOS (*Breaded Chayotes*)

3 large chayotes	Fat for frying
1 egg, beaten	2 tablespoons grated cheese
1 cup bread crumbs	

Cook chayotes, peel and slice. Dip slices into egg, roll in crumbs and fry in deep hot fat (370 degrees F.) until golden brown. Before serving sprinkle with grated cheese. Yield: six servings.

CHAYOTES DE QUERÉTARO (*Chayotes, Querétaro-Style*)

2 tablespoons flour	1 teaspoon chopped parsley
2 tablespoons butter	Salt and pepper to taste
½ cup milk	6 chayotes
2 hard-cooked eggs, chopped	½ cup buttered bread
4 carrots, cooked and chopped	crumbs

Brown the flour with butter, add a few tablespoons water and when the liquid begins to simmer add milk and cook slowly until thickened. Add eggs, carrots and parsley and season with salt and pepper. Cook the chayotes, drain and remove a slice from the top of each, taking care not to separate it entirely. Hollow out centers, chop centers very fine and blend with fried mixture. Fill chayotes shells with stuffing and cover with buttered crumbs. Replace chayote lid and bake in a moderately hot oven (375 degrees F.) for fifteen to twenty minutes. Yield: six servings.

CHAYOTES A LA VERACRUZANA (*Chayotes, Veracruz-Style*)

1 clove garlic, sliced	4 cooked chayotes
3 tablespoons olive oil	½ chili Jalapeño, diced
2 onions, chopped	(Page 238)
4 large tomatoes	6 green pitted olives
2 teaspoons chopped parsley	

Fry garlic in oil until browned. Add onions, tomatoes which have been peeled and chopped, parsley and the chayotes which have been peeled and diced. Cover and cook over a low fire for ten to twelve minutes. Before serving add the chili and olives. Serve alone or with a meat course. Yield: six servings.

PERITAS DE CASTAÑAS (*Chestnut Croquettes*)

1 cup thick white sauce	Salt
2 cups ground cooked chestnuts	Pinch of pepper
	2 eggs, beaten
4 tablespoons sugar	½ cup bread crumbs
2 teaspoons agua de azahar, or ½ teaspoon vanilla	Fat or salad oil

Mix well the first four ingredients. Add salt and pepper and chill for several hours or overnight. Divide mixture into eight portions and shape into cones or balls. Dip the croquettes into the beaten egg and then into the bread crumbs so that the outer surface is completely covered. Fry in deep hot fat (370 degrees F.). Serve very hot. Yield: eight servings.

RAJAS CON QUESO (*Chilies and Cheese*)

4 large sweet peppers	3 tablespoons shortening
4 medium-sized tomatoes, peeled	1 teaspoon salt
	½ pound cream cheese, sliced
2 medium-sized onions, chopped	

Hold peppers directly over flame for a minute or two. Peel and chop with tomatoes. Fry onions in shortening until golden brown. Add pepper-tomato mixture, one-quarter cup hot water and salt and cook slowly. When it begins to boil, add cheese and simmer slowly for about ten minutes. Yield: six servings.

CHILES EN NOGADA ESTILO PUEBLA
(*Chilies in Nut Sauce, Puebla-Style*)

6 sweet peppers, peeled and
  seeded
1 pound pork loin
Salt
1 medium-sized onion, finely
  chopped
2 cloves garlic, finely
  chopped
1 cup walnuts or pecans,
  ground
2 tablespoons fat
3 sprigs parsley, finely
  chopped
1 apple, peeled, cored and
  chopped

2 peaches, peeled and diced
1 teaspoon powdered
  cinnamon
½ teaspoon powdered
  cloves
½ teaspoon pepper
½ teaspoon thyme
1 tablespoon sugar
¼ cup sherry wine
½ cup cream cheese
1 broiled garlic clove,
  minced
¼ teaspoon cumin
½ cup milk, approximately
Seeds of one pomegranate

Make a lengthwise incision in peppers and fill with the
following stuffing: Cook pork with one and a half cups water
and one teaspoon salt till tender. Drain, reserving stock, and
chop very fine. Fry onion, garlic and half the ground nuts
in the fat. Add stock in which meat was cooked and simmer
ten minutes. Add chopped meat, parsley, apple, peaches, cinnamon, half the cloves, the pepper, thyme, sugar and wine
and simmer five to ten minutes or until stock has evaporated.

Mix together well the remaining nuts, cream cheese, broiled
garlic, cloves, cumin, salt to taste and the milk, adding more
if needed to make a thin sauce. Pour over the peppers and
garnish with pomegranate seeds. Yield: six servings.

RAJAS CON CREMA (*Pepper Strips with Cream*)

6 sweet peppers
3 tablespoons butter

1 teaspoon salt
1 cup cream

Remove skins and seeds from peppers and cut into narrow strips lengthwise. Fry in butter four or five minutes or until tender. Add salt to the cream and pour over the peppers. Cook one or two minutes longer over a low flame. Yield: eight servings.

CHILES RELLENOS (*Stuffed Peppers*)

4 *large green peppers*	2 *citrons, chopped*
2 *onions, chopped*	6 *large green olives, chopped*
½ *pound ground pork meat*	*Salt and pepper to taste*
1 *tablespoon lard*	*Flour*
1 *tablespoon raisins*	2 *eggs, separated*

Hold peppers over flame two minutes, turning them to expose entire surface. Wrap in a napkin, leave about ten minutes and peel. Cut peppers lengthwise, remove seeds, wash, sprinkle with salt and stuff with the following mixture:

Brown onions and pork in lard. Add raisins, citrons, olives, salt, pepper and one-fourth cup water. Mix well and cook over a very slow fire for about twenty-five minutes. Sprinkle peppers with flour. Beat egg whites and yolks separately and fold together. Dip peppers in egg and fry in deep hot fat (350 degrees F.). Yield: four servings.

MAJARRETE (*Corn Pudding*)

12 *ears tender corn*	1 *tablespoon butter*
1 *quart milk*	2-*inch stick cinnamon*
1¼ *cups sugar*	1 *teaspoon powdered*
3 *egg yolks, beaten*	*cinnamon*

Cut kernels of corn from cobs, grind and stir into milk. Strain and add sugar. Mix egg yolks and corn mixture. Add butter and cinnamon stick and cook over low heat, stirring constantly, about twenty minutes or until it attains a custard consistency. Turn onto a platter and sprinkle with cinnamon. Yield: six to eight servings.

TORTA TABASQUEÑA DE ELOTE
(*Corn Casserole, Tabasco-Style*)

12 ears corn	2 eggs, beaten
½ cup butter	½ teaspoon salt
1 cup sugar	

Grind the corn kernels and then add butter which has been creamed with sugar. Mix well, add eggs and salt and pour into a buttered casserole. Bake in a moderate oven (350 degrees F.) thirty minutes. Remove from oven when a knife inserted in the center comes out clean. Serve cold. Yield: six servings.

EUCHEPOS (*Green Corn Tamales*)

6 ears tender corn	2 sweet peppers, peeled,
1½ teaspoons salt	diced
½ cup butter	1 cup cream

Cut kernels from cobs and grind. Reserve leaves. Add one teaspoon salt. Wash corn leaves well and in each leaf place one heaping tablespoon of the ground corn. Fold the leaf well about the mixture. Cook in a covered double boiler for about fifteen minutes. Remove mixture from corn leaves, slice and fry in butter with the sweet peppers until golden brown. Serve with hot cream to which one-half teaspoon of salt has been added. Yield: eight servings.

TAMALES DE ELOTE (*Sweet Corn Tamales*)

6 large ears sweet corn	3-ounce package cream
1 cup butter	cheese
4 tablespoons sugar	¼ cup milk, optional
1 teaspoon salt	

Cut kernels from ears of corn and grind. Cream butter and combine with corn, sugar, salt and cream cheese. Add a little milk if corn is not tender. Mix well. Place a heaping tablespoon of the mixture on each corn leaf, fold leaf around it and pile in layers in a pressure cooker. Cook at fifteen pounds pressure about thirty minutes. Yield: two to two and one-half dozen tamales.

TORTA DE PAPAS (*Potato Casserole*)

2 pounds potatoes	2 teaspoons grated lemon
1 cup butter	rind
1 cup granulated sugar	4 eggs, well beaten

Peel potatoes, boil until tender and press through a sieve. Add the butter, sugar, lemon rind and eggs. Turn into a buttered baking dish and bake in a moderate oven (350 degrees F.) twenty-five minutes or until the pudding is a golden brown. Yield: six servings.

GORDITAS DE PAPA (*Potato Patties with Guacamole*)

3 large potatoes, boiled	½ cup shortening
½ cup corn meal	1 cup cooked chicken,
2 ounces grated cheese	shredded

Sieve potatoes and mix with corn meal and cheese. Mold into patties and brown in very hot shortening. Cover with chicken. Serve with guacamole sauce. Yield: six servings.

Guacamole Sauce

3 avocados	Salt and pepper to taste
2 tomatoes, peeled	3 slices of bacon, fried
1 onion, chopped	slowly, crumbled
2 small chilies serranos	
(Page 238)	

Peel avocados and mash to a smooth consistency. Add bacon crumbs and tomatoes, which have been chopped very fine and drained, onion and chilies. Season with salt and pepper. Yield: six servings.

TIMBALITOS DE ESPINACA (*Spinach Timbales*)

2 *pounds spinach, cooked*	1 *teaspoon chopped onion*
2 *tablespoons butter*	*Salt and pepper to taste*
2 *tablespoons cream*	6 *strips bacon*
2 *raw eggs*	2 *hard-cooked eggs*

Drain spinach and chop very fine. Mix with butter, cream, raw egg, onion, salt and pepper. Grease small molds with butter and fill with the mixture, pressing it solidly. Place molds in a pan of hot water and bake in a moderate oven (350 degrees F.) twenty minutes. Turn mixture out of molds onto a hot platter and place on each one a strip of cooked bacon and slices of the hard-cooked eggs. Yield: six servings.

TORTAS DE FLOR DE CALABAZA (*Squash Flower Fritters*)

18 *squash blossoms*	3 *large tomatoes, peeled,*
3-*ounce package cream*	*drained*
cheese	2 *tablespoons chili powder*
2 *tablespoons flour*	1 *medium-sized onion,*
3 *eggs, separated*	*chopped*
¾ *cup shortening*	

Remove stems and pistils of blossoms. Wash well and cut in halves lengthwise. Place three halves one on top of another and then add a slice of cheese. Add another layer of three halves and sprinkle with flour. Make six of these "sandwiches."

Beat egg whites, then yolks and fold together. Dip the flower sandwiches into the beaten eggs and fry in half-cup shortening. Fry remaining ingredients in the other one-quarter cup of shortening about eight minutes. Put the flower sandwiches in this mixture and allow to simmer over very low heat ten minutes. Yield: six servings.

CALABACITAS EN NOGADA (*Zucchini in Nut Sauce*)

6 large zucchini	2 pomegranates
½ small head cauliflower	1 tablespoon chopped
2 tablespoons olive oil	parsley
2 tablespoons vinegar	⅓ cup almonds, blanched
Salt and pepper	½ cup walnuts
2 small avocados, diced	6 tablespoons bread crumbs
Powdered cinnamon	2 tablespoons sugar

Boil zucchini in a small quantity of salted water until tender and drain. Cut in halves lengthwise and remove centers. Reserve shells. Cook cauliflower until tender, drain, and chop. Fry cauliflower two or three minutes in olive oil. Add a tablespoon vinegar, salt, pepper, avocados, pinch of cinnamon and the seeds of one pomegranate. Fill the zucchini shells with the mixture, place on a platter and cover with nut sauce. Sprinkle with pomegranate seeds and parsley.

To make nut sauce, chop almonds and walnuts. Add bread crumbs, one-quarter cup water, sugar, one tablespoon vinegar and a pinch of salt. Mash and mix thoroughly. Yield: six servings.

CALABACITAS SUREÑAS (*Zucchini, Southern-Style*)

6 medium-sized zucchini	¼ pound pork, diced and
2 onions	fried
3 tomatoes	Salt and pepper to taste
2 sweet green peppers	1 cup grated cheese
¼ cup fat	

Wash zucchini and dice. Peel and chop onions, tomatoes and peppers. Add zucchini and fry in fat over low heat, covered, until the zucchini is tender, about fifteen minutes. Add pork and season with salt and pepper. Before serving sprinkle with grated cheese. Yield: six servings.

SALADS

But, there are so few salads—that has been the lament of any number of people trying to work out Mexican menus for northern tastes. The reason is that Mexicans eat a large variety of fruits and vegetables but plain or prepared in other ways—in desserts, soups or as elaborately-styled vegetable courses. Actually, many dishes have built-in salads—tostadas compuestas, for example, and tacos dorados. Therefore salad at a Mexican meal, which invariably includes a plate of flowered radishes, olives, chilies and pickled onions, seems almost unnecessary.

There are some traditional salads, however, and these like soups are indicative of both the imaginativeness and the desire for substance in Mexican kitchen thinking. The one time that salad becomes a main dish is on Christmas Eve. Then families sit down together after the midnight mass to eat the colorful and solid beet salad of the Noche Buena.

In recent years Mexican cooks and housewives in the city have also evolved a number of fine salads from northern influences but of exclusively Mexican ingredients. The most popular salad food is the avocado. This is used in a number of ways from a simple affair of cubed avocado on a leaf of lettuce served with lemon and tomato sauce to the elaborate stuffed avocado.

The Mexicans were the first to find that the avocado makes a fine accompaniment for sea food like shrimp and crabs, and some of the best of the local salad productions are a combination of these.

Like most interesting salad ingredients, the avocado is a native "fruit," which was prized long before the coming of the Spaniards. In both Mexico and Peru, pre-Conquest pottery has been discovered in the shape of avocados and there are a number of varieties produced locally—some weighing only a few ounces, others as much as four pounds.

A few other favorite salad ingredients of local origin are radishes, the small squash or zucchini and peppers. Chili originally meant cool or cold and was used to designate the big sweet peppers, but the Spaniards used it as a generic term to cover every conceivable shape, size and variety. The big sweet peppers are important in salad making, but invariably salads are spiced with the smaller ones, even the "devil" peppers of the Mayans, which the children of Yucatan eat with such relish. A popular salad vegetable is the chayote or the christophine which is much favored in the southern part of the United States. In Mexico it is eaten sliced or mashed or made into a vegetable pudding.

Although most Mexicans prefer to eat fruit raw or candied, a number of interesting salads have been concocted from the fruits which abound there and which are also of local origin—the papaya, mangoes, bananas, apples, strawberries, tuna, the all-purpose cactus, and in first place, the pineapple.

AGUACATES RELLENOS (*Stuffed Avocado Salad*)

6 avocados
½ cup cooked or canned
    sweet corn, drained
½ cup peas, cooked
½ cup cooked string beans,
    chopped
1 large head lettuce

2 tablespoons olive oil
1 tablespoon vinegar
1 tablespoon mustard
1 teaspoon salt
1 teaspoon pepper
3 tablespoons mayonnaise

Peel avocados, cut in half lengthwise and remove stones. Mix corn, peas, string beans and six or eight outer leaves of lettuce, finely chopped. Add olive oil, vinegar, mustard, salt and pepper, and mix well. Stuff avocados with salad mixture. Garnish with mayonnaise and serve on lettuce leaves. Yield: six servings.

ENSALADA DE COLIFLOR (*Cauliflower Salad*)

1 large head cauliflower
1 teaspoon salt
2 tablespoons olive oil
1 tablespoon vinegar
1 teaspoon salt
½ teaspoon pepper

½ pound cooked ham,
    chopped fine
4 sprigs parsley, chopped
    fine
1 cup light mayonnaise

Break cauliflower into flowerets and cook in salted water until just tender. Drain and cool. Place in a salad bowl. Mix oil, vinegar, salt and pepper and add. Mix ham with parsley and sprinkle over cauliflower. Cover with the mayonnaise. Yield: six servings.

ENSALADA DE CARNE (*Meat Salad*)

1 pound pork loin, cooked
½ pound pork tongue, cooked
1 cup white chicken meat, cooked
2 pigs feet, cooked
½ cup olive oil
¼ cup vinegar
1 teaspoon salt
½ teaspoon pepper
½ teaspoon marjoram
½ teaspoon thyme
½ teaspoon laurel

1 small head lettuce, chopped fine
2 medium-sized tomatoes, cut in small pieces
20 olives
10 radishes
3 avocados, peeled and sliced
1 canned chilpotle, sliced (Page 238)
3-ounce package cream cheese, sliced thin

Chop together the cooked meats. Mix oil, vinegar and seasonings, add to meats and allow the mixture to stand for three hours. Before serving, mix in lettuce and tomatoes. Garnish with olives, radishes, avocados, chilpotle and cheese. Yield: twelve servings.

ENSALADA DE CHAYOTE (*Chayote Salad*)

3 good-sized chayotes
1 teaspoon salt
3 tablespoons olive oil
1 tablespoon vinegar

½ teaspoon salt
½ teaspoon pepper
1 onion, sliced

Cook chayotes about twenty minutes in salted water. Peel, chill and cut into small squares. Place on salad plates and pour over a dressing made of olive oil, vinegar, salt and pepper. Garnish with onion. Yield: six servings.

CHILES RELLENOS DE SALMON (*Peppers Stuffed with Salmon*)

1½ cups canned salmon, drained
4 avocados, peeled and mashed
2 teaspoons salt
¼ cup olive oil
6 small onions, chopped
2 small green pickled peppers, chopped
1 teaspoon chopped parsley
1 teaspoon chopped cilantro (optional)
6 large sweet green peppers
¼ cup vinegar
2 tablespoons Worcestershire sauce
1 teaspoon pepper

Chop salmon, mix with avocados, one teaspoon salt, two tablespoons olive oil, one onion, pickled peppers, parsley and cilantro. Peel large peppers, remove seeds and soak in the vinegar, other teaspoon of salt, and remaining oil for at least two hours. Drain soaked peppers and stuff with salmon mixture. Place on a serving dish and sprinkle with a sauce made by blending mixture in which the peppers were soaked, with Worcestershire sauce and pepper. Chill thoroughly. Yield: four to six servings.

ENSALADA DE PIÑA Y MANZANA (*Pineapple and Apple Salad*)

4 good-sized apples
1 tablespoon lemon juice
1 cup chopped pineapple
½ teaspoon salt
1 tablespoon vinegar
4 tablespoons sugar
¼ cup sherry wine

Peel apples, core and chop. Add lemon juice and then other ingredients and toss together in a salad bowl. Yield: six servings.

ENSALADA POBLANA (*Puebla Salad*)

3 large potatoes, cooked   1 teaspoon French mustard
1 cup parsley   1 egg yolk
1 bunch scallions   1 cup diced celery
1 tablespoon melted butter   Salt and pepper to taste

Chop or slice potatoes and place in a salad bowl. Boil
parsley and scallions about five minutes, drain, cool, chop
and mash. Mix butter, mustard, egg yolk and diced celery.
Add to potatoes and season to taste. Yield: six to eight
servings.

ENSALADA DE RABANOS (*Radish Salad*)

2 cups radishes, chopped   ½ teaspoon pepper
½ cup vinegar   2 tablespoons capers
3 teaspoons salt   1 canned chili Jalapeño,
4 tablespoons olive oil   cut into strips (Page 238)

Soak radishes in vinegar and two teaspoons salt for three
hours and drain. Mix vinegar with olive oil, remaining salt
and pepper and pour the dressing over radishes. Garnish
with capers and chili. Yield: six servings.

ENSALADA DE CAMARONES Y AGUACATE
(*Shrimp and Avocado Salad*)

2 avocados   3 tablespoons olive oil
2 canned pimientos   1 tablespoon vinegar
1 cup (¾ pound) canned or   1 teaspoon salt
  cooked shrimp, drained   ½ teaspoon pepper

Peel and dice avocado. Chop pimientos and mix with
avocados and shrimp, in a salad bowl. Combine other four
ingredients and pour over the salad. Yield: four servings.

ENSALADA DE CALABACITAS Y AGUACATE
(*Squash and Avocado Salad*)

6 *fat, round zucchini,*	4 *tablespoons olive oil*
parboiled	1 *tablespoon vinegar*
2 *avocados, peeled and sliced*	6 *mint leaves, chopped*
6 *scallions, cooked*	*Salt and pepper to taste*
1 *stalk celery, finely chopped*	*Lettuce*

Cut slice from top of each zucchini and scoop out the insides. Mix remaining ingredients, stuff zucchini and serve on lettuce. Yield: six servings.

ENSALADA DE VERDURAS (*Vegetable Salad*)

3 *carrots, cooked*	3 *sprigs parsley, minced*
1 *large turnip, cooked*	1 *tablespoon capers*
3 *potatoes, cooked*	4 *tablespoons olive oil*
½ *cup string beans, cooked*	2 *tablespoons vinegar*
1 *small head cauliflower,*	1 *teaspoon salt*
cooked	½ *teaspoon pepper*
12 *olives, chopped*	

Chop carrots, turnip, potatoes and beans and mix. Place the whole cauliflower in the center of a deep serving dish and surround it with the chopped vegetables. Sprinkle with olives, parsley and capers and pour over all a dressing which has been made by blending olive oil, vinegar, salt and pepper. Yield: six servings.

ENSALADA DE CALABACITAS (*Zucchini Salad*)

2 *pounds zucchini*	½ *teaspoon salt*
1 *teaspoon salt*	1½ *ounces cream cheese,*
3 *egg yolks*	*or 1½ ounces mild*
1 *teaspoon dry mustard*	*American cheese, sliced*
½ *cup olive oil*	*thin*
½ *cup vinegar*	3 *hard-cooked eggs, sliced*
½ *teaspoon pepper*	

Scrub zucchini well and cut off ends, do not pare. Cook covered, in one inch of boiling water with salt twenty minutes or until tender. Drain, cool, cut in halves and place in a serving dish.

Blend egg yolks and mustard in oil and vinegar. Pour over the zucchini, sprinkle with salt and pepper and garnish with cheese and hard-cooked eggs. Yield: six servings.

Chapter 9

Desserts and Confections

"IT's AS GOOD as if made by a nun's fingers" is still the crowning compliment for a food and particularly for a dessert in Mexico. The reason is that most of the candies and desserts of Spanish origin, like turrón, reached perfection in convents where the nuns carefully continued the Spanish cuisine. Cooking was considered an art among the religious women, along with embroidery and needlepoint; and they specialized in making desserts and candies which were sent as gifts to dignitaries and which were also often sold to bring revenue to the convent.

Desserts brought by the nuns from Spain and made in Mexico for centuries were much influenced, like the architecture, by the Moorish domination of Spain. The East is evident in the thick pastes and in the heavy delicately flavored sweets. These are more like candy than the familiar northern desserts and are meant to be taken in minute quantities with the meal.

Some of the desserts for which various convents won fame were the Ante de Almendras, Turrón de Yemas, the sweet spongy Huevos Reales—all of Spanish origin, but now considered Mexican. Spanish methods were adapted to the foods at hand. The vast abundance of Mexican fruits, particularly the coconut inspired the Old-World cooks. Coconut in any form is one of the favorite sweets of Mexico, and the cries of vendors can be heard summoning the people at all hours to the perambulating stands where chunks of coconut are displayed on pyramid shelves. More than one hundred different kinds of candies are made from the meat and the milk and all sorts of legends have grown up about the coconut, including stories of the frightening bogey man who is El Coco.

A delicious coconut dessert is the Queso de Coco. This "cheese" is prepared of only a few basic ingredients. It is actually eaten like cheese at the end of the meal but in infinitesimal portions with an apple or other fruit, or perhaps some salted crackers.

Other desserts grew out of Mexico's lush tropical fruits, enriched with Spanish flavor. Papaya, a favorite which is eaten for breakfast and drunk as a refresco, is also served in a heavy syrup for dessert as are bananas, pineapples, apples.

The need to preserve fruits against the ravages of the tropical climate led to the popularity of a molded jam called Ate, with high sugar content. The fruit is peeled and cooked with an equal amount of sugar until transparent. Then it is poured for storage into little boxes. Ates will keep for months, even years, without losing freshness or flavor. They are delicious served at the end of a meal in slices and sometimes with a light cheese.

Ates are the special contribution of Michoacan, which is one of the most beautiful states in Mexico with mountain ranges sweeping across the state. It has been noted for its artistry since the first Tarascans established their kingdom on the shores of the lake and called it Tzintzuntzan, the Place of the Hummingbirds.

Mexico is also indebted to Michoacan for one of the two national desserts. Chongos were conceived in a small pleasant town named Zamora on the way to Guadalajara. They are favored by rich and poor alike and are both a fiesta and everyday dessert. They may be bought canned, but with a little time and a little care are easily prepared at home.

The other national dessert is Flan.

One of the most popular figures in all Mexico is the flan vendor. You will hear his sweet and slightly melancholy call at all hours of the day, in all parts of the country. It may be at six o'clock in the morning in the narrow cobbled streets of Orizaba or at three in the afternoon in a little Aztec village, or even later in the evening in the capital, as he trudges along swinging from his hand the glass box with its quivering burden of gelatinas in jewel colors or the rich deep gold of the flan.

The sweet potato is another traditional basis for desserts. The rich roots are cooked in a heavy cinnamon-flavored syrup until candied. Then they are molded into the long thin strips to make camotes which constitute a Puebla fame. A delicious puddinglike dessert is made by cooking them in a syrup of sugar and orange juice. After mashing, they are served with whipped cream, flavored with kirsch, and sprinkled with nuts, candied fruits and raisins.

In an old section of Mexico City, beside the elaborately carved façade of the palace of a former grandee, stands a Mexican sweetshop with a fabulous array of more than three hundred kinds of delicacies. There are candied lime peels stuffed with coconut cooked in syrup; almond paste cunningly molded into little animal figures; soft marshmallowlike rolls coated with nuts; candies of every imaginable form and combination of ingredients.

Mexicans have always been fond of sweets. Babies acquire a desire for sweet things sucking on the bits of sugar cane given to appease them. The main dishes of the Aztec meals were followed by elaborate courses of sweetmeats and pastries for which the Aztec cooks achieved fame—and with no more to go on than maize flour, eggs, honey, sugar and spices. It is rather curious that the flavors of chocolate and coffee, so much a part of other dessert and candy recipes, have not been stressed. In Mexico they are usually considered beverages and are taken so in great quantities during the day.

Like the desserts, many of the sweets are based on recipes brought from Spain and the greater part are of Arabic origin. They are exceedingly heavy.

A famous basic sweet is the leche quemada or burned milk. This is simple and emphasizes the use of essential foods. To make it, milk is cooked slowly, sugar added and the mixture stirred constantly over a low fire for hours until it thickens and becomes caramel-colored. The sweet has dozens of variations. It is flavored with the famous Papantla vanilla, cinnamon or wine, and ground nuts or fruits are frequently added.

Convents became as famous for candies as for desserts. At the Santa Rosa convent in Puebla, whose kitchen is now a national monument, the nuns concocted the wonderful camotes made of candied sweet potatoes. At the convent of San Francisco in Mexico City, the nuns were noted for the Aleluyas—hallelujahs—made of almonds, milk, sugar and cinnamon. They received their name from the fact that they were always given as presents on Easter.

Nut candies are also very popular, particularly those of almond, peanut and piñon.

Come high prices, wars, droughts and other disasters, there is one group of persons in Mexico who have only the most secure thoughts about mañana—the three hundred and more families who make and sell the candied fruits, the taffy, the sweets made of calabash, cactus fruit, milk and sugar in the candy market in Mexico City.

ANTE DE ALMENDRAS (*Almond Dessert*)

Probably because they have been so deeply influenced by Spain, the colonial cities of Puebla and Guanajuato and Queretero cling, as they have for centuries, to the ways of cooking which were of the homeland. Although many convents throughout the country triumphed in one dish or another, the convents of these three places were famous for good food. The Puebla almond dessert is one of the finest and until the convents were closed by the government, everyone with a sense of good living and affection for a friend sent to the convent regularly for some of the almond dessert for a Saint's day or an anniversary remembrance.

1½ cups sugar
½ cup water
⅓ cup sweet sherry wine
½ cup blanched almonds

3 egg yolks, slightly beaten
4 slices sponge cake, three-quarters inch thick

Boil sugar and water together five minutes. Remove from heat and divide into halves. Add sherry to one half. Combine almonds with the other half and add egg yolks. Cook almond mixture about five minutes or until it thickens, stirring constantly. Cut sponge cake into two-inch squares. Soak squares in wine syrup. Arrange a layer of the sponge cake in a buttered casserole (about six by two inches). Pour a layer of the egg and almond mixture over the cake and cover with some of the wine syrup. Repeat procedure in layers until all the ingredients have been used. Bake in a slow oven (325 degrees F.) until top is brown or about twenty-five minutes. Cool and turn out on a plate. Serve cold but not refrigerated the following day. Yield: six servings.

QUESO DE ALMENDRAS (*Almond Mold*)

One of the important contributions to Mexican cookery which the Spaniards brought with them was almonds. Almonds give tantalizing flavor to a host of dishes—fish, fowl, meat and vegetables. But, they are at their most glorious in desserts. Queso de almendras is a case in point. It is also graphic proof of how a few simple ingredients are cunningly combined into a dish fit for a king. Queso de almendras like other "cheeses" in the dessert file should be brought to the table on a *best* platter and cut into individual portions about the size of a bisque Tortoni.

1½ cups sweet almonds, blanched	1½ cups sugar
	6 egg yolks, beaten
1 egg white	Powdered cinnamon

Mix almonds and egg white and grind. Boil together sugar and one cup water, stirring, until sugar is dissolved, to 236 degrees F. (soft ball in cold water). Add almond paste and egg yolks. Simmer gently, stirring constantly, till bottom of pan can be seen. Pour into a ring mold without a bottom which has been set upon greased waxed paper. Let stand until firm. Remove ring and cover entire surface with a thick coating of cinnamon. Yield: six servings.

PERONES DE HUEVOS REALES (*Apples with Royal Eggs*)

Although most apples in Mexico, particularly the familiar rosy varieties from the northern states, are called "la manzana," there is a variety grown in Central Mexico and in the Federal District which is distinguished by its color and texture. "El perón" is the name given to them: their masculine gender setting them apart and above the other fruit. Mounds of the chartreuse-colored apples can be seen piled on the floor of any small Indian market or arranged with geometric artistry on the sidewalks by street vendors. The firm hard green cooking apples of New England and the Northern United States make an excellent substitute.

6 green apples	3 eggs, beaten
1 cup sugar	1 pint milk
1 tablespoon lemon juice	1 teaspoon vanilla
3 tablespoons raspberry jam	3 ounces macaroons,
2 tablespoons butter	crumbled

Peel and core apples. Bring to a boil one-half cup sugar, one-half cup water and lemon juice. Add apples and simmer until almost tender. Remove apples to a greased baking dish, fill cavities with jam and top with a bit of butter. Blend eggs and remaining one-half cup sugar. Add milk, vanilla and macaroons. Mix and pour around apples. Bake in a slow oven (300 degrees F.) for about one hour, until custard is firm. Yield: six servings.

DULCE ZACATECAÑO (Zacatecano Banana Dessert)

3 large bananas, not too ripe	½ cup heavy sweet cream
5 tablespoons butter	¼ cup dry sherry wine
¼ cup sugar	1 teaspoon vanilla

Peel bananas and slice lengthwise. Sauté in butter until golden brown. Drain on paper and place in a shallow baking dish or pie plate. Sprinkle with a little sugar. Whip cream, add remaining sugar, wine and vanilla. Pour over bananas, covering them completely. Chill and serve very cold. Yield: six servings.

DULCE DE FRIJOL (*Bean Dessert*)

1 cup small red beans,	*2½ cups scalded milk*
soaked	*1¼ cups sugar*
2 cups water	*2-inch stick cinnamon*

Simmer beans in water two to three hours or until tender. If a pressure cooker is used, allow only a cup of water and cook at fifteen pounds pressure sixty minutes. Drain and mash. Mix with milk and sieve. Add sugar and cinnamon. Cook over high heat, stirring constantly, until mixture begins to boil. Boil five minutes, then lower heat and let the mixture cook until it thickens, one hour or longer. Stir constantly until bottom of the saucepan can be seen. Yield: six servings.

CAPIROTADA (*Bread Pudding*)

8 slices stale white bread	*3 ounces hard cheese,*
¾ cup lard	*crumbled*
1 cup brown sugar	*6 tablespoons butter*
1 stick of cinnamon	*⅓ cup pine nuts*
	½ cup water

Fry bread in hot lard. Cook sugar, cinnamon and one-half cup water until syrupy, about five minutes. Arrange bread in layers with syrup, cheese, bits of butter and nuts. Brown in a slow oven (325 degrees F.) and serve very hot. Yield: six servings.

TUNA DELICIA (*Cactus Fruit Delight*)

6 cactus fruits	*1 teaspoon cinnamon*
¼ cup powdered sugar	*3 teaspoons anisette*

Peel fruits and place on a serving dish. (They are obtainable in cans.) Sift the sugar with cinnamon and sprinkle over fruit. Pour half a teaspoon of anisette over each fruit. Chill thoroughly. Yield: six servings.

TORREJAS (*Cake Slices in Syrup*)

3 eggs, separated and beaten
6 slices sponge or pound
cake three-quarters inch
thick
3 tablespoons butter
2 cups sugar

1 cup water
½ cup sweet sherry wine
5 cloves
2-inch stick cinnamon
3 candied figs, sliced
18 candied cherries

Fold egg whites into yolks. Dip slices of cake in eggs and fry in butter until light golden brown. Boil sugar in water till syrupy. Add sherry, cloves and cinnamon and simmer five minutes. Put cake slices into syrup and simmer four or five minutes. Serve in deep dish and garnish with figs and cherries. Yield: six servings.

CHONGOS JALAPEÑOS (*Little Knots, Jalapa-Style*)

2 cups sugar
6 egg yolks, beaten
2 tablespoons butter

½ pound sponge cake
4 tablespoons grated cheese
1 cup water

Add one cup of water to the sugar and boil over low heat fifteen or twenty minutes or until a heavy syrup is formed. Remove and cool. Add beaten egg yolks and heat again for five minutes, stirring constantly. Remove from fire and add one tablespoon butter. Grease a baking dish with the rest of the butter and lay three half-inch slices of cake on the bottom. Pour half the syrup over the cake and sprinkle with half the grated cheese. Repeat layers. Bake in a moderate oven (350 degrees F.) ten to twelve minutes or until the top is golden brown. Yield: six servings.

QUESO DE COCO (*Coconut cheese*)

1 cup sugar
¼ cup water
1 cup (4-ounce can) grated
  coconut

2 egg yolks, well beaten
Cinnamon

Add sugar to water and cook, stirring, until sugar is dissolved. Add coconut and cook slowly, stirring, about five minutes or until mixture forms a thick paste. Cool. Add egg yolks and cook very slowly, stirring constantly, about fifteen minutes or until the mixture is very thick. Remove from heat, stir three to four minutes, press into a shallow round mold and chill in the refrigerator. Unmold and sprinkle lightly with powdered cinnamon. Serve in small pieces with apples or salted crackers. Yield: six servings.

DULCE DE COCO (*Coconut Dessert*)

2 large coconuts, grated
2 cups sugar

6 egg yolks, beaten
1 cup water

Cook together coconut, coconut milk and one-half cup water, stirring constantly about ten minutes. Drain by pressing well in a napkin (about one cup of juice should be obtained). Mix juice with syrup made by boiling sugar with one-half cup water seven or eight minutes. Add the egg yolks and cook, stirring constantly, fifteen or twenty minutes or until the mixture takes on the consistency of marmalade. Yield: ten servings.

BIEN ME SABE DE LECHE DE COCO
(*It-Tastes-Me-Well Coconut Dessert*)

4 coconuts
2 cups sugar
1 cup water

10 egg yolks, well beaten
Cinnamon

Peel coconut meat, grind and press in a muslin bag to extract the milk. Boil sugar and water to 236 degrees F. (soft ball in cold water). Add coconut milk and egg yolks to syrup and cook over low heat, stirring constantly, about ten minutes. Pour into a shallow serving dish, sprinkle with cinnamon and serve cold. Yield: twelve to fifteen servings.

COCADA (*Coconut Dessert*)

1 cup sugar
1 cup cold water
1 cup fresh (or 4-ounce can) shredded coconut

4 egg yolks, slightly beaten
2-inch stick cinnamon

Boil sugar in coconut milk or, if canned coconut is used, in one cup of water ten minutes or until the mixture is syrupy. Add coconut and boil slowly, stirring often, fifteen minutes. Cool a little and slowly add, stirring, egg yolks and cinnamon. Place over high heat and boil, stirring constantly, about thirty minutes or until the bottom of the pan can be seen. Pour mixture into a greased seven-inch baking dish and brown lightly in a slow oven (325 degrees F.). Serve cold on a dessert platter. Yield: six servings.

CREPAS CON CAJETA (*Crêpes with Caramel Sauce*)

½ cup sifted all-purpose flour
½ teaspoon salt
1 tablespoon grated lemon rind

2 eggs, well beaten
⅔ cup of milk
1 tablespoon melted butter
Cajeta de Celaya (page 189), or canned cajeta

Combine flour, salt and lemon rind. Mix eggs, milk and butter, add to the flour mixture and beat until smooth. For each crêpe, pour a little less than one-quarter cup on a hot greased griddle, tilt the griddle to spread thinly. When lightly browned, turn and brown lightly on other side.

To serve, spread with cajeta, roll, sprinkle with confectioners sugar. Yield: ten crêpes or five servings.

FLAN DE ALMENDRAS (*Almond Custard*)

1 can sweetened condensed
  milk
1 cup almonds, toasted,
  ground

6 egg yolks, beaten
4 tablespoons sugar
⅓ cup blanched almonds
1 cup water

Bring one cup of water to a boil. Add condensed milk and ground almonds and simmer three minutes. Cool. Add egg yolks slowly, stirring constantly. Put sugar in a baking dish, sprinkle with two tablespoons water and heat till sugar is caramelized. Rotate to coat inner surface of dish. Cool slightly. Fill dish with custard, place in pan of water and bake in slow oven (325 degrees F.) thirty minutes. Garnish with blanched almonds. Yield: six servings.

FLAN DE LECHE (*Milk Custard*)

1 quart milk
½ to ¾ cup sugar
4 egg yolks, beaten lightly

2 egg whites, beaten lightly
¼ cup brown or powdered
  sugar

Sweeten milk to taste and cook over low heat, stirring often, until it has the consistency of a smooth custard. Cool and add yolks and whites which have been combined. Stir well.

Carmelize custard cups by dusting them thickly with brown or powdered sugar and putting them in a hot oven. Move the molds from side to side so that the entire inner surface of each is covered with caramel. Pour custard into the molds and place in a pan of water. Bake in a slow oven (300 degrees F.) about one hour, or until a silver knife inserted in the center comes out clean. Chill overnight in the molds. To serve turn out onto dessert plate. Yield: six servings.

FLAN SUPREMO (*Custard Supreme*)

1 pound chestnuts
½ cup sugar
2 cups milk, scalded

3 eggs, lightly beaten
1 teaspoon vanilla

Wash chestnuts and cut a cross in each through the top and far down the sides. Bake in a very hot oven (500 degrees F.) fifteen minutes. Take off shells and skin, boil twenty minutes in water to cover, drain and grind. Mix chestnuts with remaining ingredients and beat until thoroughly blended. Pour into a baking dish or into individual molds and set into a shallow baking pan of hot water. Bake in a slow oven (300 degrees F.) about one hour, or until a silver knife inserted in the center comes out clean. Remove at once from water and cool quickly and thoroughly. Serve plain or with a sauce. Yield: six to eight servings.

FLAN TROPICAL (*Tropical Custard*)

1 pound sugar
¾ cup almonds, blanched and ground
6 eggs, well beaten
1 teaspoon flour

1 tablespoon butter
1 teaspoon brandy
1 teaspoon dry white wine
1 teaspoon lemon juice
1 cup water

Bring to a boil slowly sugar and one cup water. Add almonds and cook two minutes. Remove from fire and add, stirring, beaten eggs. Add flour which has been creamed with butter, brandy, wine and lemon juice. Pour mixture into buttered baking dish and bake in a moderate oven (375 degrees F.) until brown or about twenty miutes. Yield: six or eight servings.

CHONGOS ZAMORANOS (*Little-Knots Milk Dessert*)

1 quart milk	2 cups white sugar
1 egg yolk, beaten	2 tablespoons brown sugar
2 rennet tablets	2-inch stick cinnamon
⅛ teaspoon salt	

Heat milk to lukewarm. Add egg yolk, blend and strain. Dissolve rennet tablets and salt in about three tablespoons of cold water and add to milk and egg mixture. Stir and set in a warm place about twenty minutes or until junket forms. Cut into two-inch squares or smaller if desired. Place the squares carefully one at a time in a deep saucepan, separating one from another and set over a low flame.

Dissolve the sugars in one cup of water and when the junket squares begin to bubble, add a cupful of the sugar mixture and the cinnamon. Pour it carefully around the edges of the pan in order not to break the squares. Add more syrup to junket as syrup thickens until all the syrup has been added. Simmer over very low heat about forty-five minutes or until the syrup is thick. Serve very cold in small sherbet dishes or ice cream plates. Yield: six servings.

CAJETA DE CELAYA (*Caramelized Goat's Milk Sauce*)

5 quarts milk (goat's if available), scalded	1 large stick cinnamon
	¼ cup cornstarch
1 teaspoon soda	½ cup water
2⅔ cups sugar	½ cup sherry wine

Bring to a boil over low heat milk, soda, sugar and cinnamon. Blend cornstarch in a few tablespoons of cold milk. Add to the milk mixture, stirring constantly. Cook, stirring, until the bottom of the pot can be seen when scraped with a spoon. Add water, mixing it thoroughly, then add sherry and cook, stirring constantly, until the bottom of the kettle can be seen again. Pour the mixture into small wooden boxes or glasses. If desired, in place of the starch a full cup of ground blanched almonds may be used Yield: four quarts. (Cajeta de Celaya, most famous of the many varieties; portions are sold in little wooden boxes, specially made for them, and are sent all over the Republic and to many foreign countries. The soft caramel is eaten plain, is served on bread or a spoonful is stirred into a glass of milk. Although much more substantial than most of the toppings served in the U.S., it is delicious with ice cream.)

DULCE RAPIDO (*Quick Dessert*)

4 egg yolks	*¼ cup brandy*
⅓ cup almonds, blanched and ground	*4 egg whites, stiffly beaten*
¼ cup sugar	*1 tablespoon powdered sugar*
½ cup milk or light cream	*1 teaspoon powdered cinnamon*

Beat egg yolks with almonds and sugar for ten minutes. Add milk slowly, then brandy and three beaten egg whites. Pour into dessert or cocktail glasses, filling them about three-quarters full. Beat powdered sugar with remaining beaten egg white and place a spoonful on top of each glass. Sprinkle with cinnamon. Yield: six servings.

HUEVOS REALES (*Royal Eggs*)

This is another of the purely Spanish dishes which has been adopted ingredient by ingredient in Mexico and is now considered part of the national cuisine. In Spain, the dish is known as Huevos Chimbos. In Mexico, it is simply Royal Eggs. Although the age of progress now sees them bottled for sale on the shelves of Super-Mercados and delicatessens, no real gourmet would ever dream of affronting the regal nature of the dish with ready-made labels.

8 egg yolks	4 tablespoons raisins
1¼ cups sugar	4 tablespoons blanched
2-inch stick cinnamon	almonds
½ cup sweet sherry wine	4 tablespoons pine nuts

Beat the egg yolks until thick and pale lemon-colored. Pour into a small casserole, cover, set in a pan of water and bake in a moderate oven (350 degrees F.) thirty minutes or until puffy and firm. Cool and cut into one-inch squares.

Add the sugar and cinnamon to half cup of water and boil five minutes. With a spatula, carefully place the egg squares in the syrup. Let them soak in the simmering syrup. When the squares are saturated, take them out one at a time with the spatula and place in a serving dish. Strain the syrup, add the wine and pour over the squares. Chill, garnish with the raisins and nuts. Serve at once, or the following day when the flavor will have improved. Yield: six servings.

DULCE DE HIGOS (*Preserved Figs*)

Select figs that are green and very hard. Prepare a mild lime solution by boiling one-half tablespoon lime in one gallon water, stirring until it stops bubbling, and allow it to settle. When clear, pour over figs, which have had a small slit cut in the blossom end of each fig. Boil until figs are tender. Drain, drop in ice-water and leave overnight. In the morning, gently press water out of each fig and wash thoroughly in clear water until the taste of the lime has thoroughly disappeared. For each cup of figs, make the following syrup: Boil one cup of sugar and one-half cup of water till syrupy. Add figs and cook until very tender. A one-inch piece of ginger root may be added for flavor. Fig preserves will keep indefinitely if sealed in jars when hot.

GUAYABAS RELLENAS (*Stuffed Guavas*)

| 16 large guavas | 6 medium-sized apples |
| 1 pound sugar | ½ cup finely chopped nuts |

Peel guavas and soak in cold water one hour. Drain, cut in half and scoop out seed and pulp. Cook shells in water to cover for five minutes over low heat or until guava shells are tender. Remove and place shells in cold water. Bring to a boil sugar and one pint of water. Add guava pulp and simmer over low heat until syrup has been reduced to one-half the original amount. Peel apples, core and quarter. Add water to cover, bring to a boil and drain. Add apples to the guava syrup and cook slowly until the mixture forms a paste. Stuff the guava shells with paste and fit two halves together so that the fruit appears whole. Chill thoroughly. Serve sprinkled with nuts. Yield: eight servings.

BUÑUELOS (*Crisp Pastries with Syrup*)

2 eggs, beaten	*¾ teaspoon salt*
1 cup milk	*1 teaspoon baking powder*
4 cups flour	

Blend eggs and milk. Sift together dry ingredients and add to egg-milk mixture. Roll dough as thin as possible, cut into rounds seven inches in diameter and fry in deep hot fat (370 degrees F.) until a delicate golden brown. Serve hot with the following syrup. Yield: eight servings.

Wine Cinnamon Syrup

6 tablespoons sugar	*½ cup white wine*
½ cup water	*½ teaspoon cinnamon*

Combine ingredients and boil until syrup is formed.

PASTEL DE FRUTAS (*Fruit Cake*)

2 candied orange peels	*1 candied sweet potato or*
4 candied lemon peels	*equal amount candied fruit*
4 candied peaches	*8 candied figs*
1 slice candied cactus fruit	*1 cup sugar*
12 quarter-inch slices	*1 cup water*
sponge or pound cake	*½ cup rum*

Dice the candied fruits or cut into thin strips. Place a layer of three or four cake slices on the bottom of a deep dish. Add a layer of candied fruits. Cover with another layer of cake and another layer of candied fruits. Repeat until ingredients are used. Dissolve the sugar in one cup of water and pour over the layers. Then add the rum. Press down, cover dish and allow it to stand twenty-four hours in a cool place. Remove cake from dish, unless serving dish has been used, and place on serving dish. Cover with custard sauce.

Custard Sauce

2 tablespoons sugar	1 pint milk, scalded
1½ tablespoons cornstarch	1 teaspoon vanilla
2 egg yolks	

Mix sugar with cornstarch and egg yolks. Add milk, stirring and cook over low heat, stirring, for about five minutes or until thickened. Cool quickly and add vanilla. Yield: six servings.

DULCE DE MANGO (*Mango Dessert*)

1 cup water	1 teaspoon vanilla
2 cups sugar	6 large ripe mangoes

Boil together water, sugar and vanilla over low heat thirty minutes. Peel and slice mangoes, add to syrup and simmer until the syrup is condensed to one-quarter the original amount. Serve very cold. Yields six servings.

DULCE DE PAPAYA VERDE (*Candied Green Papaya*)

All through the late summer and early fall, in the capital and in little towns and villages throughout the Republic, mounds of papaya wait at any city street stand for a buyer. Typically native, papaya is the most popular of all fruits in Mexico. Papaya is eaten for breakfast, cold, and served with lemon juice. Papaya is eaten for the slender evening meal. Papaya juice and papaya whip and papaya "infusions"— papaya-flavored fruit drinks of all varieties—are best sellers in the cities and the villages. One of the more elaborate and one of the best ways of preparing it is this dessert made of green papaya.

¼ cup lime	2 cups sugar
½ medium-sized green papaya	2 or 3 fig leaves

Soak the lime in about two quarts of water for one hour. Allow it to settle and then strain. Add papaya which has been peeled and cut into two-inch squares and let stand overnight. Remove papaya, wash and simmer lightly in fresh water to cover about ten minutes. Cool. Press the pieces of papaya gently between thumb and forefinger to remove any excess moisture.

Boil together sugar and two cups of water stirring till sugar is dissolved and mixture forms a thread. Add papaya and fig leaves. Simmer gently over very low heat about twenty minutes. Remove the papaya pieces and place on a serving dish. Chill thoroughly. Although it has a somewhat candy-like quality, this sweet is served as a dessert to be eaten with a fork. Yield: six servings.

ARROZ DE LECHE I (*Rice Pudding I*)

⅓ cup rice	2 egg yolks, lightly beaten
1 cup water	⅓ cup seedless raisins, washed
1 teaspoon salt	
Rind of one lemon, grated	3 tablespoons butter
3 cups milk	1 teaspoon powdered cinnamon
2-inch stick cinnamon	
1 cup sugar	

Soak the rice in enough hot water to cover for fifteen minutes. Drain and wash well in cold water. Cook in one cup of water with salt and lemon rind. When the water is absorbed and the rice is fluffy, add milk and stick cinnamon and simmer fifteen minutes. Add sugar and cook slowly for ten minutes longer. Remove from heat, while stirring, add egg yolks and raisins and cook, stirring often, five minutes longer or until the mixture has attained a custard-like consistency. Add the butter and stir until cool. Serve sprinkled with cinnamon. Yield: six servings.

BUDIN DE ARROZ II (*Rice Pudding II*)

1 quart milk	*2 tablespoons walnuts or*
½ cup raw white rice,	*pecans, ground*
washed	*4 eggs*
Rind of one quarter lemon	*2 egg yolks*
1¼ cups sugar	*1 cup raspberry marmalade*
4 tablespoons grated	*or jelly*
coconut	

Heat milk to boiling, add rice and lemon rind. Cook over low heat twenty-five minutes or until tender, stirring now and then to prevent sticking. Remove lemon rind. Add one cup sugar, coconut and nut meats. Add the whole eggs and egg yolks one by one, beating constantly. Caramelize remaining sugar, add enough water to make a syrup and pour into a baking dish. Add custard. Set the dish in an outer pan of water and bake in a slow oven (325 degrees F.) about two hours or until rice is done. Cool, turn out of baking dish and cover with marmalade or jelly. Yield: six to eight servings.

DULCE DEL SUR (*Southern Sweet*)

½ cup butter	*⅜ cup flour*
½ cup powdered sugar	*½ teaspoon baking powder*
½ teaspoon cinnamon	*2 tablespoons raisins*
Rind of one half lime	*2 tablespoons pine nuts*
2 eggs	*¼ cup cream*
½ cup corn meal	

Melt butter, cool and add sugar, cinnamon and lime rind. Beat well. Add eggs one at a time and continue to beat briskly. Sift together corn meal, flour and baking powder and add to butter mixture blending well. Add raisins, pine nuts and cream and mix thoroughly. Pour into buttered custard cups and bake in a moderate oven (375 degrees F.) twenty minutes. Before serving, sprinkle with additional powdered sugar. Yield: six to eight servings.

DULCE DE CALABAZA (*Squash Sweet*)

1 squash, ripe not yellow	*1 gallon water*
½ tablespoon lime	*Sugar*

Cut squash into two by four inch strips and remove seeds. Boil lime in water, stirring, until it stops bubbling and allow it to settle. When clear pour over squash to cover and allow it to stand overnight. Remove squash and wash thoroughly in water, until all taste of lime is gone. Boil in fresh water, until tender, but not soft. Drop at once into ice cold water and then drain, and weigh. Use two cups sugar and one cup water for each pound of squash. Boil together sugar and water till syrupy, add squash and boil slowly until syrup is thick and squash has achieved a brittle consistency. This sweet will keep for several weeks in a cool place.

ATE DE CAMOTE Y PIÑA (*Sweet Potato and Pineapple Paste*)

2 pounds sweet potatoes, cooked	*2 pounds sugar*
	2 cups ground pineapple

Peel and grind sweet potatoes, taking out all coarse fibers, or force through a colander. Heat together sugar and one-half cup water, stirring until sugar is dissolved. Add sweet potatoes and simmer fifteen minutes, stirring constantly. Add pineapple and continue to cook slowly until mixture is very thick and the bottom of the pan may be seen when scraped with a spoon. Remove, cool and mold into a loaf. Serve on a platter garnished with almonds and raisins. Yield: three pounds.

HUEVITOS DE FALTRIQUERA (*Colonial Candy*)

2 cups sugar
8 egg yolks, beaten
4 ounces almonds, blanched
  and ground
½ teaspoon cinnamon

¼ teaspoon powdered
  cloves
¼ cup powdered sugar
Colored tissue or waxed
  paper

Boil sugar in one cup water fifteen minutes or until a thread is formed. Cool and add egg yolks, almonds, cinnamon and cloves. Cook over low heat ten minutes, stirring constantly. Remove from heat and continue stirring until firm. Spread powdered sugar lightly on a platter and turn the mixture onto the sugar. Mold in small balls and wrap each in tissue paper. Yield: about two dozen "little eggs."

YEMITAS (*Egg Candy*)

1 pound sugar
10 egg yolks, lightly
  beaten

2 tablespoons powdered
  sugar
1 teaspoon powdered
  cinnamon

Dissolve sugar in one cup water and boil to 236 degrees F. (soft ball in cold water). Remove and allow to cool until it is tepid. Add egg yolks while stirring. Cook very slowly, stirring, until a thick paste is formed or about fifteen minutes. Pour into a shallow dish and cool. Mold into little balls the size and shape of an egg yolk. (*Yema* is the Spanish word for yolk.) Sprinkle each well with powdered sugar mixed with the cinnamon. Yield: about one and a half pounds.

DULCE DE HIGOS (*Candied Figs*)

1½ pounds green figs   1½ pounds sugar
1 tablespoon salt

Scrape the figs with pumice stone and place them in a pot
with one quart of water and salt and bring to a boil. When
the water has begun to boil, remove from the heat for about
a half minute. Return to the heat and bring to a boil again.
Remove. Repeat this procedure four times. Drain and wash
the figs well in warm water to remove the salt. Rinse two or
three times. Remove stems from figs and make little cross
cuts at the end. Put sugar in a pot with one cup of water and
bring to a boil over a low heat. Add the figs and simmer
gently for ten minutes. Let them stand twenty-four hours in
the syrup. Boil again for another ten minutes. Let stand again
and repeat process. By this time the figs should be transparent. Yield: about two and a half pounds.

CONSERVA DE GUAYABA (*Guava Conserve*)

20 large fresh guavas   2 pounds sugar

Peel the guavas. Dissolve sugar in one quart of water in a
pewter pot and boil for six minutes over moderate heat. Add
guavas and simmer slowly for five minutes. Remove from
fire and let stand for twenty-four hours. Repeat operation on
two successive days.

ATE DE GUAYABA (*Guava Paste*)

2 large cans of guavas   2 pounds sugar

If guavas come whole, cut them in halves and remove
seeds. Place the seeds in a dish and put the guavas in a bowl.
Add one cup of water to seeds, allow to stand ten minutes

and pass through a sieve. Grind the guavas. Mix the guavas and the strained water in a heavy pot, preferably of pewter, copper or earthenware. Add sugar and place over low heat, stirring constantly with a wooden spoon. Cook until the bottom of the pan can be seen in the wake of the spoon. Pour into a loaf pan about one-inch deep and allow to harden, preferably in the sun, until it is completely dry on top. This will take four or five days. It will keep for months if stored in a cool place. In Mexico it is generally made one year for use the next. If fresh guavas can be obtained use two pounds. Yield: about two and one-half pounds.

DULCE DE LIMONES (*Candied Limes*)

2 dozen large green limes   *1½ cups sugar*

Scrape the limes and slash each with a long vertical cut. Soak in cold water for three days, changing the water morning and evening. Each time the water is changed squeeze the limes slightly and gently. After they have soaked for the requisite time, bring sugar and three-fourths cup water to a boil. Add limes and simmer slowly about fifteen minutes. Remove and let stand until the following day. Boil again for fifteen minutes and again on the third day. Limes should be transparent. Yield: two dozen candied limes.

MAZÁPAN (*Marchpane*)

2 pounds sugar   *9 egg yolks, well beaten*
1 pound blanched almonds,
ground

Boil the sugar with one-fourth cup of water to a very heavy syrup. Add almonds and egg yolks, and cook over low heat stirring constantly, about fifteen minutes or until a pinch will not stick to the fingers. Cool the paste, spread it on a

damp napkin and roll as a jelly roll. Cover with a piece of
paper and dry in a very slow oven for a few minutes. Yield:
ten servings.

MAZAPÁN DE ALMENDRA (*Marchpane of Almonds*)

2 pounds blanched almonds   2 pounds sugar
15 bitter almonds

Grind the sweet and bitter almonds together, adding about
one-fourth cup of water when grinding. Put the sugar in a
pan with one-fourth cup of water and boil to a very heavy
syrup. Add the ground almonds. Stir constantly over a low
fire until a pinch of the mixture between the thumb and forefinger will not stick, about fifteen minutes. Remove from
fire and pour into baking pan lined with paper. Smooth the
top with a knife. Dry in a very slow oven (300 degrees F.)
for a few minutes. Yield: ten servings.

TURRÓN DE YEMAS (*Nougat*)

1 cup sugar   6 egg yolks
¾ cup blanched almonds
   ground

Boil sugar and an equal amount of water to 236 degrees
F. (soft ball in cold water). Add almonds and well beaten
egg yolks. Cook, stirring, over low heat about ten minutes
or until the mixture thickens. Remove and stir until cool.
   Serve quite cold on a dessert dish ornamented with leaves.
Yield: six servings.

TIRILLA DE DURANZO (*Peach Candy*)

2 cups fresh sliced peaches   2½ cups sugar
1 tablespoon salt

Soak the peach slices in one quart of water with salt for four hours. Rinse in cold water, drain and place in a saucepan with sugar over very low heat. Let simmer slowly until the peaches acquire a jelly-like consistency. Remove carefully and lay peach strips on tray. Set in the sun for several days. The candy will keep for a year.

BOLITAS DE NUEZ (Pecan Candies)

1 cup pecans, ground   1 egg white, stiffly beaten
½ cup powdered sugar

Mix the pecans with the sugar and add the egg white. Form into small balls and bake on a buttered pan in a moderate oven (350 degrees F.) five minutes. Yield: about eight servings.

CONDUMIO DE CACAHUATE (Peanut Candy)

3¾ cups sugar   2 pounds shelled peanuts,
                                  unsalted and chopped

Mix the sugar with two cups of water and bring to a boil, stirring over low heat. Continue cooking to 236 degrees F. (soft ball in cold water). Add the peanuts, remove from fire and beat thoroughly. Pour into very shallow buttered pan, cool and cut into squares. Yield: about three and a half pounds candy.

DULCE DE LECHE (Milk Candy)

12 egg yolks   ½ cup butter
1 cup sugar   2 tablespoons powdered
2 cups sifted flour   sugar
1 cup milk   1 teaspoon powdered
Grated rind of two limes   cinnamon

Mix egg yolks with sugar and add the flour. Pour in the milk, slowly, stirring constantly to avoid lumps. Add the grated rind of limes and the butter in little chunks. Cook over low heat for twenty minutes, stirring constantly. When the mixture is thick enough so that the bottom of the pan can be seen in the wake of the spoon, pour into a shallow pan. Cut into small strips and deep fry till lightly browned. Drain each strip as it is taken out of the hot fat. After about two minutes sprinkle with sugar which has been sifted with cinnamon. Yield: about twelve servings.

Chapter 10

Breads, Cakes and Cookies

OVENS ARE NOT NECESSARY, but they are nice.

For centuries the Aztecs and the Mayans had gone along in much the same way their descendants do in the rural areas today with kitchen equipment essentially consisting of three stones, in the center of which was the hearth fire. A large clay griddle called a comal rested on the stones for cooking tortillas. Other adjuncts included the metate, or slanting stone for grinding corn, and the *metlapil,* a stone rolling pin tapering at the ends. There were also pottery dishes and containers of beautiful and dazzling design, the molinillo or wooden beater used to whip chocolate, and the *molcajete,* a pottery bowl with a rough-ridged bottom for grinding chilies, tomatoes, and onions and herbs.

This was satisfactory equipment, as anyone who has ever eaten the simple foods will testify. Tortillas are still the standard "bread." In the northern states they are made of flour, but in most of the Republic the simple corn mixture is eaten as it was before the Spaniards arrived. Still a festive food as it was when the corn goddess was honored is the "gordita"—a little cake cooked on braziers set up on street corners on cold evenings. These chunky little rounds of corn meal, sugar, and eggs are a traditional food during the great December celebration to honor the Virgin of Guadalupe, whose shrine—the holiest in Mexico—stands on the site once occupied by the temple of the Aztec goddess of Earth and Corn.

Since the arrival of the Spaniards, however, no fiesta day has been complete without oven-baked bread. The Spaniards brought ovens with them and pastry secrets which quickly captured the affection of the peoples of Mexico. They brought imagination to the basic Spanish recipes, and bread soon became the most varied and the most widely used of all Mexican foods.

Breads are, for the most part, bought from the baker, whereas tortillas are usually cooked at home. A familiar sight on any Mexican street is the bakery boy on his bicycle, whizzing surely beside long lines of new-model cars. He is completely overshadowed by the huge straw basket on his head filled with crisp golden bolillos, the softer broader teleras used for tortas, long loaves of twisted bread, simple sticks.

More popular and more varied than ordinary bread is the pan dulce or sweet bread. Chocolate and pan dulce or coffee and pan dulce constitute for most people the merienda or light evening meal. In Mexico there are more than one hundred different kinds of pan dulce, each with its own name and its own devotees. There are huge puffs sprinkled with sugar, tiny twisted sweet rolls, pastry-like squares and triangles. A trip to a bakery is an adventure; each customer takes a tray and a pair of tongs and is welcome to spend as much time as he wishes picking and choosing the particular combination that will make breakfast or the light evening meal a gourmet's treat. In restaurants, at almost any hour of the day when a cup of coffee is ordered it comes to the table accompanied by a basket of sweet bread. When making up the bill, the waiter or waitress makes a quick count of the contents and levies the tariff according to the number missing.

In addition to this huge assortment for everyday, there is special bread for many occasions. On Hallowe'en, the Day of All Souls, round loaves decorated with cross bones and coated with anise sugar-syrup are baked to gladden the hearty appetites of Los Muertos. The famous Rosca de Reyes—Bread of the Magi—with its burden of gifts is always part of the January sixth festivity.

A requisite of any village festival is the "pan" of the region, molded into animals, flowers and little figures with names fashioned on the surface and sometimes mottoes. Markets everywhere are brightened by the men and boys walking through the crowds with huge trays of yellow bread balanced on their heads, and even the most speed-mad bus driver will stop amiably for purchases to be made through the bus window.

But breads are only part of the tradition. The Spaniards brought to Mexican food a richness as Churrigueresque as their architecture. It expressed itself completely in both fields. The beautiful and elaborately adorned museum in Puebla is called the "sugar paste" house and, like so many of the baked products, it has a feathery fairylike quality for all of its substantiality.

Breads and sweet breads are the stock in trade of the bakery shops. But there are also pastelerías or pastry shops where cakes of every description may be purchased and where delicious cookies and other desserts abound. Hazelnuts, almonds and walnuts are widely used in making cakes and cookies and the wide variety of native fruits has also been incorporated and some of the spices—particularly sesame.

Some other forms of pastry are much liked: churros—long sugared melt-in-the-mouth pastries much like crisp crullers; the simulated chicharrones which are sweet; buñuelos, wafer-thin and saturated with syrup and frequently covered with nuts and raisins, the powdery polvorones and there is even a recipe for "sighs," the suspiros, which are no more than egg yolks, sugar and a little flour puffed to an airy thought in an oven.

MOLLETES (*Biscuits*)

2 eggs
6 tablespoons butter, melted
¼ pound nixtamalina
    (packaged or canned), or
    ¼ pound white corn
    meal

1 cup flour
2 teaspoons cream of tartar
1 teaspoon baking soda
½ cup milk
6 tablespoons sugar

Beat egg whites, then yolks and fold together. Add the warm melted butter. Add the nixtamalina or white corn meal and the flour, sifted with the cream of tartar and baking soda. Mix well and add the milk slowly until a soft dough is formed. Place rounded spoonfuls on a greased cookie sheet and sprinkle liberally with sugar. Bake in a moderate oven (375 degrees F.) fifteen to twenty minutes or until light brown. Yield: four dozen.

CHICHARRONES FINGIDOS (*Mock Cracklings*)

4 egg whites	3 cups shortening
3 cups sifted flour	6 egg yolks
¼ cake or package of yeast	1 cup brandy

Beat egg whites with one tablespoon flour until stiff. Add the yeast which has been dissolved in two tablespoons water. Cream one cup shortening. Add egg yolks, egg white mixture, flour and brandy, and mix well to a soft dough. Bake in a greased loaf pan in a moderate oven (350 degrees F.) thirty to forty minutes or until done. Cool and cut into one-eighth inch slices. Deep-fry in remaining hot shortening (350 degrees F.) until golden brown. Yield: four or five dozen.

AREPAS (*Griddlecakes*)

2 cups sifted flour	3 tablespoons sugar
1 egg yolk	2 tablespoons powdered
½ cup shortening	sugar
1 teaspoon powdered aniseed	1 tablespoon cinnamon

Sift flour three times into a deep bowl. Add the egg yolk, shortening, anis and sugar. Mix well. Pat into little pancakes about one-half inch thick and two inches in diameter. Sprinkle with powdered sugar and cinnamon which have been mixed together. Bake in a slow oven (325 degrees F.) until golden brown. Yield: two to two and one-half dozen.

BIZCOCHUELOS (*Sweet Bread*)

1 package yeast	½ cup shortening
1½ cups sugar	2 eggs, well beaten
2 cups lukewarm water	1 teaspoon salt
6 cups flour	1 teaspoon aniseed

Dissolve yeast and two tablespoons sugar in warm water. Stir in three cups flour. Beat until mixture is smooth. Allow sponge to stand in a warm place (about 85 degrees F.) two hours. Add shortening and remaining sugar which have been creamed together, eggs, salt, aniseed and the rest of the flour. Knead on a floured board until smooth and elastic. Place in a greased bowl in a warm place (about 85 degrees F.) until light and double the original size, or about two hours. Knead again and let stand thirty minutes. Knead again and shape into loaves. Place in greased loaf pans and brush tops with melted butter. Let rise again until double in bulk. Bake in a hot oven (425 degrees F.) for ten minutes, lower temperature to slow (325 degrees F.) and bake about fifty minutes longer. Yield: 2 loaves.

MOLLETES DE CALABAZA (*Pumpkin Muffins*)

1 cup cooked and strained
   pumpkin
¾ cup milk
1 egg, well beaten

1½ cups flour
1 teaspoon salt
3 teaspoons baking powder

Mix the pumpkin and milk and when cool add the egg. Sift the flour, salt and baking powder together and add to the pumpkin mixture. Pour into greased muffin tins, filling them half full, and bake in a hot oven (425 degrees F.) thirty minutes. Yield: about ten muffins.

MOLLETES DE ARROZ (*Rice Muffins*)

1 egg, beaten
1 cup milk
1 cup cooked white rice
3 tablespoons butter,
   melted

½ cup sifted flour
3 teaspoons baking powder
½ teaspoon salt
2 tablespoons sugar

Mix egg, milk, rice and butter. Add flour sifted with baking powder, salt and sugar. Mix rapidly and fill greased muffin pans two-thirds full. Bake in a hot oven (425 degrees F.) twenty-five to thirty minutes. Yield: about one dozen.

MANTECADOS (*Butter Thins*)

1 cup butter	2 cups sifted flour
1 cup sugar	2 tablespoons powdered
6 eggs	sugar

Cream butter and sugar. Add eggs, one by one, beating after each addition. Add flour gradually and continue to beat until very smooth. Pour into two dozen muffin tins lined with paper cups, sprinkle with powdered sugar and bake in a moderately hot oven (375 degrees F.) fifteen to twenty minutes. Yield: four dozen cakes.

MARQUESOTE (*Caramel Cake*)

8 eggs, separated	1 tablespoon powdered
¾ cup powdered sugar	sugar
1 cup cornstarch	1 teaspoon cinnamon

Beat egg whites until very stiff, add beaten yolks slowly, beating after each addition. Fold in the three-fourths cup powdered sugar which has been sifted with the cornstarch. Pour mixture into a buttered and floured round baking dish about eight inches in diameter and bake in a moderate oven (350 degrees F.) about thirty minutes. To test for doneness insert a silver knife in the middle. If the knife comes out clean, the dish is cooked. Mix remaining sugar and cinnamon and sprinkle over top. Yield: six servings.

PAN CRIOLLO (*Creole Bread*)

8 eggs, separated	¾ cup butter, melted
1¼ cups powdered sugar	1 teaspoon grated lemon
1 cup flour	rind
⅔ cup cornstarch	2 tablespoons lemon juice
1 tablespoon baking powder	

Beat egg whites stiffly. Then add yolks one at a time, beating after each addition. Add the sugar and continue to beat well. Sift together flour, cornstarch and baking powder. Mix the egg-blend and add slowly butter, lemon rind and juice. Pour batter into greased muffin pans and bake in a moderate oven (350 degrees F.) for fifteen minutes. Yield: about twenty little cakes.

—

PANECILLOS BORRACHOS (*Drunken Cupcakes*)

10 eggs	½ cup plum jam or
¾ cup sugar	marmalade
1½ cups sifted cake flour	1 cup light sugar syrup
	½ cup brandy

Beat all the egg yolks and two whites until stiff. Add sugar and continue beating until thick. Add flour and fold in remaining egg whites which have been stiffly beaten. Fill greased deep muffin pans half full and bake in a moderate oven (350 degrees F.) about twenty-five minutes. Cool. Remove from pans, place on serving dish and put a teaspoon of jam or marmalade on top of each cake. Bathe with a mixture of syrup and brandy. Yield: four dozen cakes.

PASTELITOS DE CIRUELA (*Prune Cake*)

6 cups flour	1 cup water
1½ cups butter	1 cup prune marmalade
1 egg	1 egg yolk
1 tablespoon sugar	

Mix flour, butter and egg with the sugar which has been dissolved in water. Knead until it is a soft dough and divide into thirds. Roll each on a pastry board to about one-half inch thickness. Place one part in a greased deep cake pan. Spread with a thin layer of marmalade. Add another layer of dough, spread with remainder of the marmalade and cover with the final layer of dough. Blend egg yolk with one tablespoon water and brush over the top. Sprinkle with additional sugar. Bake in a moderate oven (375 degrees F.) fifty minutes or until light brown. Yield: twenty-four servings.

PAN DE RON (*Rum Cake*)

1 cup butter
1½ cups sugar
6 eggs
1 teaspoon grated lemon
   rind

1 tablespoon lemon juice
2 cups sifted cake flour
2 teaspoons baking powder
1 cup cornstarch
¼ cup rum

Soften the butter, add sugar and beat together until creamy. Add eggs, one at a time, beating well. Then add grated lemon rind and juice. Sift flour with baking powder and cornstarch. Add alternately with rum to creamed mixture, mixing all ingredients well. Pour into two greased loaf pans nine by five by three inches. Bake in a slow oven (325 degrees F.) one hour and one-half or until done. Cool on a wire cake rack ten to fifteen minutes before removing from pans. Yield: two loaf cakes.

PAN DE AJONJOLÍ (*Sesame Seed Cake*)

1½ cups sifted flour
2 teaspoons baking powder
¼ teaspoon salt
½ cup sugar

½ cup milk
1 egg, beaten
3 tablespoons melted butter

Sift together flour, baking powder, salt and sugar. Add milk, egg and butter and stir until blended. Pour into a well greased deep nine-inch baking pan and cover with almond topping.

Almond Topping

½ cup sifted flour
½ cup brown sugar
½ teaspoon powdered
 cinnamon

⅛ teaspoon salt
½ cup chopped almonds
2 tablespoons melted butter
1 teaspoon sesame seed

Mix flour, brown sugar, cinnamon, salt and almonds and slowly add the melted butter, beating well. Sprinkle mixture over the batter and sprinkle with sesame seed. Bake in a moderate oven (350 degrees F.) thirty minutes. Yield: eight servings.

POLVORONES DE ALMENDRA (*Almond Cookies*)

2 cups sifted cake flour
1 cup shortening
½ cup sherry wine

½ cup almonds, blanched,
 toasted and finely
 chopped
½ cup powdered sugar

Spread the flour in a large frying pan or on a cookie sheet and bake in a moderately hot oven (400 degrees F.) five minutes or until brown. Remove and cool. Sift flour in a mound on a pastry board and make a depression in it. Fill the depression with shortening, wine and almonds which have been mixed together. Blend thoroughly, but do not knead. Roll on a board to one-half-inch thickness and cut into rounds one and one-half inches in diameter. Place on greased cookie sheets and bake in a moderately hot oven (400 degrees F.) for twelve to fifteen minutes or until golden brown. Remove and sprinkle with the sugar. Yield: about fifty cookies.

PANECILLOS DE PLÁTANO (*Banana Cookies*)

2 cups flour
1 teaspoon salt
3 teaspoons baking powder
4 tablespoons butter, softened

¾ cup milk
2 bananas
2 tablespoons lemon juice
2 tablespoons sugar

Sift together flour, salt and baking powder. Add butter, mix well, add milk and stir only till dampened. Roll to one-half inch thickness. Cut into cookies about two inches in diameter and place on a greased cookie sheet. Slice bananas one-half inch thick, dip pieces in lemon juice and then in sugar and place a slice on each cookie, pressing it down. Bake in a hot oven (425 degrees F.) twelve minutes or until golden brown. Yield: three dozen.

POLVORONES (*Cookies*)

2½ cups sifted all-purpose
  flour
1 cup shortening
¼ teaspoon salt

½ cup powdered sugar
1 teaspoon powdered
  cinnamon

Sift flour into a mixing bowl. Make a depression in the center and add shortening, sugar, cinnamon which have been sifted together. Knead well. Roll to one-half inch thickness and cut into one inch rounds. Place cookies on greased cookie sheets and bake in a moderate oven (350 degrees F.) ten minutes. Cool before removing from pans and sprinkle with a little powdered sugar. Yield: about four to five dozen cookies.

GALLETAS DE MAÍZ (*Corn Cookies*)

1 cup shortening
1 cup sugar
4 eggs
1 pound nixtamalina
  (packaged or canned), or
    1 pound white corn
      meal

1¼ teaspoons baking
  powder
½ teaspoon salt
¼ teaspoon baking soda
1 teaspoon powdered
  cinnamon

Cream shortening and sugar. Add eggs, one by one, beating thoroughly after each addition. Mix the nixtamalina or corn meal with baking powder, salt, baking soda and cinnamon and combine with the other mixture to a soft compact dough. Roll on a lightly floured pastry board to one-fourth inch thickness. Cut into cookies and place about one inch apart on a buttered cookie sheet. Bake in a moderately hot oven (375 degrees F.) for ten to fifteen minutes. Yield: three dozen.

ROSQUILLAS (*Doughnut-Shaped Cookies*)

1¾ cups sifted flour	2 tablespoons anisette
1 cup olive oil	½ teaspoon salt
1 egg	¼ cup sugar
2 tablespoons lemon juice	

Mix flour, one-fourth cup oil, egg, lemon juice, anis liqueur and salt until a thick smooth dough is formed. Mold the dough into tiny doughnuts, about one inch in diameter and very thin. Fry in the rest of the oil. Drain well and sprinkle with sugar. Yield: about four dozen.

PUCHAS (*Mexican Doughnuts*)

8 egg yolks	¼ cup brandy
½ cup sugar	2 egg whites
2¼ cups flour	½ teaspoon lemon juice

Beat egg yolks very stiffly or until they are a pale lemon color. Sift together sugar (reserving two tablespoons) and flour and add alternately with brandy, mixing well. Sprinkle the hands with flour, form dough into a strip and shape into rings or "doughnuts" three inches in diameter. Place the doughnuts in a greased pan and bake in a moderate oven (350 degrees F.) until slightly browned.

Beat the egg whites stiffly and add two tablespoons sugar and the lemon juice. Brush upper part of doughnuts with this mixture. Replace in oven and bake for four or five minutes or long enough for the icing to dry. Yield: about two and one-half dozen doughnuts.

NAQUIS (*Miniature Doughnuts*)

1 egg	⅓ cup buttermilk
½ cup sugar	2 cups sifted flour
1 pinch of baking soda	Fat for deep frying
½ teaspoon salt	

Mix all ingredients to form a soft dough. If necessary add a little more milk. Shape into tiny doughnuts and fry in hot deep fat (350 degrees F.). Drain on unglazed paper. Yield: three dozen.

HOJUELAS (*Fried Cakes*)

2 cups flour	½ teaspoon salt
6 egg yolks	Fat for deep frying
1 teaspoon shortening	1 cup sugar
Grated peel of one orange	2-inch stick cinnamon

Mix the first five ingredients and knead till smooth. Roll to about one-fourth inch thickness and cut into strips about one inch wide and three inches long. Fry in deep hot fat (350 degrees F.) until golden brown. Place on a serving dish and pour over them a light syrup made by boiling the sugar with one-half cup of water and cinnamon about five minutes. Yield: two dozen.

GAZNATES (*Fried Cakes*)

2 cups sifted all-purpose flour	2 cups shortening
6 egg yolks, beaten	1 cup powdered sugar
¼ cup brandy	1 tablespoon powdered cinnamon

Add flour gradually to egg yolks while beating. Knead well, sprinkling dough with brandy until it is thoroughly kneaded.

Roll into a very thin layer, cut into two-inch squares and fold by joining the upper left hand corner to the lower right hand corner. Fry in deep hot fat (350 degrees F.). Drain well and roll in sugar mixed with cinnamon. Yield: two dozen.

BIZCOCHITOS DE AVELLANAS (Hazelnut Biscuits)

1 cup hazelnuts, peeled
½ cup sugar
4 cups sifted flour

1½ cups butter
4 egg yolks

Toast nuts with sugar in a skillet. Place in a buttered pan and cool. Grind nuts and mix with the flour, butter and egg yolks until of a smooth firm consistency. Roll to one-eighth inch thickness and cut into small cookies of any shape desired. Bake in a hot oven (425 degrees F.) twelve minutes. Sprinkle with additional sugar. Yield: four dozen.

ROSQUITAS DE DAMAS (Ladies' Rings)

⅔ cup hazelnuts, blanched
¾ cup almonds, blanched
1 cup powdered sugar

2 cups flour
5 egg yolks

Toast nuts and grind. Mix all ingredients well. Form strips with the hands and shape into tiny "doughnuts." Place on a greased sheet and bake in a slow oven (325 degrees F.) eight minutes or until browned. Yield: about two dozen cookies.

GALLETAS MORELIANAS (Morelia Cookies)

1 cup flour
¼ cup sugar
2 tablespoons butter
2 tablespoons shortening

1 teaspoon baking powder
¼ cup water
1 egg yolk

Heat oven to moderate (375 degrees F.). Mix all ingredients except the egg yolk and knead lightly with the hands until the mixture has a smooth firm consistency. If necessary add one or two additional tablespoons of flour. Mold into a roll about three inches in diameter and chill. Slice into paper thin wafers and place on baking sheet. Beat egg yolk with one teaspoon water and brush over cookies. Sprinkle with additional sugar. Bake in preheated oven about twelve minutes or until golden brown. Yield: about two dozen cookies.

MUEGANOS (*Fried Almond Balls in Syrup*)

8 eggs	½ teaspoon cinnamon
1¼ cups almonds, blanched	½ cup cake crumbs
2 cups sugar	Fat for deep frying
½ cup white wine	

Hard-cook six eggs, remove yolks and mash. Grind almonds and mix with egg yolks. Boil one cup sugar with one-half cup water to 236 degrees F. (soft ball in cold water). Add syrup and wine to almond mixture. Stir in cinnamon and crumbs to form a stiff dough. Mold into tiny balls about the size of a walnut. Beat whites and yolks of the other two eggs and fold together. Dip the balls in the beaten eggs and then fry in deep hot fat (350 degrees F.) until golden brown. Add to the remaining cup of sugar one cup of water and boil to a thick syrup. Put the fried balls in the syrup and cook over very low heat thirty minutes or until almost all of the syrup has been absorbed. Yield: six servings.

PANECILLOS (*Round Cookies*)

2 cups sifted flour	¼ cup olive oil
½ cup sugar	¼ cup seedless raisins
1 egg	½ cup pine nuts or
1 tablespoon lemon juice	chopped pecans

Mix flour, sugar, egg, lemon juice, olive oil and chopped raisins to a smooth dough. Mold into little balls, the size of a walnut, and place on greased cookie sheets. Sprinkle with pine nuts and additional sugar and bake in a moderate oven (350 degree F.) twenty to twenty-five minutes. Yield: three dozen.

GALLETAS DE AJONJOLÍ (*Sesame Seed Cookies*)

4 cups flour	*3 eggs*
¼ teaspoon baking soda	*2 tablespoons aniseed*
1 cup sugar	*¼ cup milk*
1 cup shortening	*½ cup sesame*

Sift flour with soda on a pastry board. Form a mound and make a depression in the center. Place in the depression sugar, shortening, two eggs and the anis which has been soaked in three tablespoons boiling water. Mix ingredients in the center with the hand and then mix in the flour. Blend well but do not knead. Add milk slowly, mixing to a smooth dough. Roll to about one-eighth inch thickness and cut into cookies. Place on a buttered cookie sheet and brush with remaining egg which has been lightly beaten. Sprinkle heavily with sesame. Bake in a moderately hot oven (400 degrees F.) for ten to twelve minutes. Yield: two to two and one-half dozen.

Chapter 11

Fiesta and Special-Occasion Dishes

EVERYDAY, somewhere in Mexico, there is Fiesta.

It may be one of the great national holidays like the Sixteenth of September when the zocalo or socle in the capital is a vast sea of excited nationals waiting for the bell to toll and for the President to come out on the balcony of the Palacio Nacional to repeat the cry uttered by the patriot priest and which led to Mexico's independence. It may be no more than a small celebration to honor the dead hero of a village.

Fiesta may be a matter of religion. It may be the Day of the Virgin of Guadalupe when pilgrims come from all over the country to worship at her shrine in Tepeyac, or Easter, or the Noche Buena. It may be a small celebration to honor the patron saint of the village or a community Mass to the Virgin of the Candelaria in February to request help with the crops.

Whether patriotic or religious, national or in a tiny village, it is true, somewhere every day in Mexico there is fiesta. There are dancers—the concheros in huge feathered headdresses weaving tirelessly before the shrine of the Virgin of Los Remedios or the National Palace; voladores flying dizzily from precarious poles near the old pyramid of El Tajín; grotesque and comic dancers like the Little Old Men of Michoacan. Somewhere, every day, people are clad in fiesta best—the beautiful white garments of Papantla, the gay embroidered dresses of Veracruz, the ornate and exquisite fashions of the tall and lovely Tehuanas.

Fiesta in Mexico means dancing, markets aglow with mountains of fruit and displays of handicrafts, fireworks popping during the day and lighting the evening sky with brilliance. Fiestas are banners flying from cantinas, masses and processions.

Fiesta is also taken quite literally in Mexico to mean "feast."

Among the most direct and charming expressions of this fact are the fiestas given in small villages where a celebration gives the man elected sponsor a chance to share his world's goods with his neighbors. The cause may be a house-raising, or a promise made to thank a saint. Whatever, the sponsor considers it a matter of dignity and pride to offer the most and the best, and whether or not he can actually afford it, he manages to provide the chickens and the pigs for the tamales which will be served with chocolate in the early morning hours.

A particularly gay time in Mexico is the Christmas season. This begins on December sixteenth when the first of nine posadas is given. In this charming old custom, which represents the search of the Holy Family for shelter, the invited gather at a nearby house and form a procession headed by two children carrying a litter with replicas of the Holy Family. The children are followed by the other guests, each carrying a candle and chanting the posada song. When they arrive at the fiesta, they are first refused admission and a long dialogue is carried on musically. The host finally permits them to enter when they say that Mary is with them and in search of lodging. Once inside there is more singing and dancing. Sweet tamales and the delicacies which are part of all festive occasions are served and the climax comes with the breaking of the piñata. One of the children is blindfolded, given a stick to smash the clay olla covered with elaborate paper decorations and release the candy and sweets and presents inside.

Although posadas are generally family and neighborhood affairs, in some small towns like San Miguel Allende the whole population celebrates together. One of the most interesting Christmas fiestas is in Oaxaca on December twenty-third when the Feast of the Radishes is celebrated. There the plaza is jammed with small stalls to sell buñuelos, the wafer-thin sweet pastries served in heavy syrup on the Oaxaca glazed dishes. It has been the long standing custom to smash the plate when the buñuelo is eaten.

Posadas end on Christmas Eve. After the midnight Mass each family goes home to its private feast and to eat the Noche Buena salad, colorful with beets, and delicious with other vegetables, fruits and nuts.

Such a splendid time is not surrendered lightly and Christmas goes on until January sixth. During those days, everyone calls on friends for buñuelos, tamales of pork and chicken and sweet tamales, made with coconut and fruits, which are served with chocolate. On the sixth of January, the festive dish is Rosca de Reyes—Bread of the Kings—which is laden with favors and contains the doll which means that whoever finds it in his piece must sponsor the February second Baile de Compadres.

Carnival season is important everywhere, but the gayest celebrations are held in the port cities of Veracruz, Acapulco and Mazatlan—where cooks outdo themselves in the preparation of fish plates and sweetmeats—and in Merida, the lovely White City of Yucatan.

After Carnival, Mexico settles down to the Lenten season, but actually the "fasting" is almost as good as the feasting, with the small breads of the Lenten season, stuffed and savory with sea food; with eggs delicately blended with nopal leaves; and with capirotada, the rich succulent "bread pudding."

Easter is gaiety after the Passion Plays of Good Friday. It begins actually on Saturday morning when the "Judas Men"—grotesque figures of papier-mâché stuffed with gunpowder—begin to explode in the early dawn.

Summer means the feast of Saint Anthony when the domestic pets and animals are adorned with flowers and taken to the church door for annual blessing; the feast of Corpus Christi and charro festivals and patriotic celebrations. One of the brightest of the regional fiestas of the summer is that held in Tehuantepec, the isthmus which is part of Oaxaca. All through the month of June each barrio or section honors its patron saint with several days of feasting, dancing, parades and fiestas, which always culminate with the throwing of fruits. Women, carrying large lacquer bowls filled with fruit, cakes and toys and decorated with bright paper climb to the roof of the church and throw fruit to the crowd below.

Weddings, death, anniversaries, graduations, planting—all days and all occasions in Mexico serve to provide the people with fiesta and fiesta foods.

CANAPÉS NAVIDAD (*Christmas Canapés*)

2 tablespoons butter	6 slices brown or whole-
½ cup ground pecans or	wheat bread
walnuts	Pickles
1 teaspoon chilpotle chili	Pickled onions
juice (Page 238)	Pickled chilies
1 teaspoon salt	

Cream butter, add nuts, chili juice and salt. Blend well. Remove crusts from bread, cut each slice into quarters and spread with nut mixture. Garnish with pickles. Yield: twenty-four canapés.

PONCHE DE NAVIDAD (*Christmas Punch*)

1 orange	2 cups sauterne, well chilled
Rind of one-half lime	2 sprigs mint, leaves only
2 tablespoons orange	½ cup hulled strawberries
liqueur	2 quarts iced soda water
¾ cup sugar	

Cut the orange in half, slice one half and peel the rind of the other half. Mix orange rind, lime rind, orange liqueur and sugar and allow it to stand, covered, two hours. Add slices of orange, sauterne, mint leaves, strawberries and finally the iced soda water. Serve at once. Yield: about twenty-five servings.

BUÑUELOS DE AÑO NUEVO I (*New Year Fried Pastries I*)

6 large hot cooked potatoes	2 egg yolks
1 cup butter	1 tablespoon flour
¼ cup brandy	2 egg whites, beaten
Salt	Fat for deep frying

Drain potatoes and pass through sieve. Mix potatoes with
butter, brandy, salt to taste, egg yolks and flour. If necessary,
add a little more flour so that the paste is moderately stiff.
Add egg whites and mix thoroughly. Drop by rounded spoonfuls in deep hot fat (370 degrees F.) and fry to a golden
brown. Drain on absorbent paper and sprinkle with cinnamon.
Yield: six to eight servings.

BUÑUELOS DE ANO NUEVO II (*New Year Fried Pastries II*)

4 eggs, separated   Fat for deep frying
4 cups sifted flour   1 cup sugar
1 cup milk

Beat egg whites and egg yolks and fold together. Add the
sifted flour. Add milk slowly, mixing thoroughly. Drop
rounded spoonfuls of the mixture in deep hot fat (360 degrees F.) and fry until golden brown. Drain. Boil sugar with
three-fourths cup water about ten minutes or until fairly
thick. Add to buñuelos. Yield: two dozen.

EMPANADAS DE HUACHINANGO
(*Lenten Bread Stuffed with Red Snapper*)

(*Special for Lenten fast days*)

3½ cups sifted flour   Water
1 egg   1 cup butter
1 tablespoon salt

Sift flour on a pastry board, make a depression in the center of the mound and place the egg and salt in the depression. Add water a little at a time and mix until dough can
be handled on the board without sticking. Allow it to stand
fifteen minutes. Then roll to one-half inch, butter the top
lightly, fold the dough and roll again. Repeat this process
five times. Chill dough about ten minutes after each opera-

tion. Then roll to about one-fourth inch and cut into pancakes about four inches in diameter. Fill each with a spoonful of filling, moisten edge with egg white, fold to form a half-moon and press edges to seal. Brush lightly with egg white and bake in a moderate oven (375 degrees F.) ten to twelve minutes or till brown. Yield: two dozen.

Filling

1 pound red snapper, filleted	3 medium-sized tomatoes,
2 cloves garlic	peeled and chopped
3 medium-sized onions,	½ teaspoon salt
peeled and chopped	½ teaspoon pepper
	½ cup olive oil

Boil fish with garlic, one onion, one tomato, salt, pepper and enough water to cover ten to twelve minutes or until dry. Heat olive oil and sauté remaining onions until transparent. Add remaining tomatoes, fry three minutes and add the fish which has been shredded. Simmer over low heat until liquid has evaporated.

PAN DE MUERTOS (Day-of-the-Dead Bread)

5¼ cups sifted all-purpose	½ teaspoon salt
flour	¼ cup orange blossom
1 package yeast	water
½ cup lukewarm water	6 eggs, separated
1 cup butter	⅓ cup milk
4 tablespoons shortening	¼ cup anisette
2 cups sugar	½ cup sugar

Sift flour and using one-third, make a mound on a pastry board. Make a depression in center, pour into the hollow the yeast which has been dissolved in the warm water. Knead well, form a ball and make incisions on the top in the form of a cross. Cover with a napkin and let the dough ferment in a warm place (85 degrees F.) until it doubles in size, one hour or longer.

Make a similar mound with the remaining flour and in the center depression put the butter, which has been creamed, the shortening, sugar, salt, orange blossom water and the egg yolks. Mix ingredients thoroughly in the center and then mix in the flour, adding the milk and anis liqueur to soften the dough. Pound dough on board and add egg whites a little at a time. Add the fermented dough and continue to beat against the board until the dough no longer sticks to it. Place in a greased bowl and allow it to stand in a warm place (85 degrees F.) until it is twice the original size. Place again on the board and pound it lightly. Divide into four portions. Separate a small ball from each portion, which will fashion the "bones" with which the bread is decorated. Shape the four large portions into rounds, sprinkle lightly with flour and let stand for five minutes. Then place on a greased and floured pan, depress each portion slightly with the hand and moisten with a brush dipped in water. Using the small portions, fashion bones and place two on each loaf in the shape of a cross. Bake in a moderate oven (375 degrees F.) forty-five minutes or until done. When cooked, glaze tops with a brush dipped in a thick syrup made by boiling the one-half cup sugar and one-quarter cup water. Sprinkle lightly with additional sugar. Yield: four small loaves.

ROSCA DE REYES (*King's Round Loaf*)

(*Exclusively for January 6*)

4 cups sifted all-purpose flour	5 eggs
½ package yeast	1 tablespoon orange blossom water
¼ cup lukewarm water	1 ounce candied citron, chopped
¼ cup butter	
¼ cup sugar	1 candied orange peel, chopped
1 teaspoon salt	
¼ cup milk	1 lemon rind, grated

Place one-third of the flour in a mound on a board and make a depression in the center. Dissolve yeast in lukewarm water and pour into center of mound, mixing it a little at a time with the flour. Knead, then form into a ball. Make two incisions forming a cross on the top of the ball and place in a floured bowl. Cover with napkin and let stand in a warm place (85 degrees F.) until it is twice its original size.

Mix butter, sugar and salt with milk and cook over moderate heat about two minutes. Pour half of the mixture into a depression made in a mound of the other two-thirds of the flour. Add two eggs and the orange blossom water. Mix thoroughly with the flour and when lukewarm add the dough which has fermented. Knead well, adding the rest of the milk mixture and two more eggs. When the dough is smooth, add citron, orange peel and lemon rind. Place in a greased pan, cover with napkin and allow it to stand twenty-four hours.

Shape dough into a large circle with a hole in the center, place on a greased baking pan and allow to stand until it has swelled almost to twice its original size. Moisten the top with a brush dipped in remaining egg, sprinkle with sugar and dot with small pieces of additional citron. Bake in a moderately hot oven (400 degrees F.) for thirty minutes or longer. Yield: one very large ring or twelve to fifteen servings.

TORTILLITAS DE VIGILIA (*Lenten Tortillas*)

4 *large tomatoes, peeled,*
  chopped and drained
2 *sweet peppers, peeled and*
  chopped
½ *cup fat*
3-*ounce package* cream
  cheese, sliced

2 *tablespoons butter*
1 *teaspoon salt*
½ *teaspoon pepper*
2 *cups cream*
12 *tortillas* (*bought*)

Fry tomatoes and peppers three minutes in two tablespoons of fat. Add half the cheese, butter, salt, pepper and cream and simmer ten to twelve minutes. Remove from heat. Cut tortillas into quarters and fry in the remaining fat until they are brown. Drain. Place the sauce back on the heat, add tortillas and simmer twenty minutes or until the sauce is very thick and almost dry. Garnish with remaining slices of cheese. Yield: six servings.

PAVO RELLENO (*Stuffed Turkey*)

1 tablespoon fat or salad oil	5 sprigs parsley
2 ounces uncooked ham, chopped fine	1 teaspoon powdered cinnamon
6 Mexican sausages, coarsely chopped	1 cup dry sherry wine
10 to 12-pound turkey	2 laurel leaves
½ pound dried apples	1 teaspoon orégano
6 ounces prunes	½ teaspoon thyme
1 ounce pine nuts	Garlic
1 tablespoon seedless raisins	Salt

Heat fat in a skillet till very hot. Add ham, sausages and turkey liver. Soak apples and prunes fifteen minutes and drain. Add to meats. Add pine nuts, raisins, parsley and cinnamon. Fry slowly fifteen or twenty minutes. Remove and add sherry and simmer slowly until the wine has evaporated. Remove and cool. Add laurel, orégano and thyme. Stuff the turkey with the mixture. Grease a roasting pan with butter. Place turkey in it, and rub with garlic and salt. Roast in a moderate oven (350 degrees F.), allowing about thirty minutes per pound. Yield: eight to ten servings.

CLEMOLE POBLANO (*Clemole, Puebla-Style*)

(*Served at village weddings and fiestas*)

1 small turkey, fowl or roaster, cut into pieces	5 chilies anchos (Page 238)
1 cup almonds, blanched and ground	½ cup fat
½ cup sesame	1 tablespoon salt
2 cloves, ground	3 tablespoons vinegar
	1 teaspoon sugar

Cover the turkey with boiling water and simmer, covered, until tender. Mix almonds with one-half of the sesame, the cloves and chilies and fry in the fat two or three minutes. Add salt. Add this mixture to the turkey and the stock in which the turkey was cooked. Add the vinegar and the sugar and simmer another twenty minutes uncovered until the sauce is moderately thick. Before serving sprinkle with the remaining sesame. Yield: twelve servings.

POLLOS FIESTA (*Chicken, Fiesta-Style*)

2 tender chickens, cut into
    pieces
4 tablespoons lemon juice
1 teaspoon salt
4 tablespoons butter
 1 small can pâté de foie gras

1 pint light cream
1 small can green peas
1 small can truffles, chopped
4 ounces cooked ham,
    chopped

Brush chickens with lemon juice and sprinkle with salt. Fry in three tablespoons butter till golden brown. Transfer to saucepan. Mix pâté and cream, add to chicken and simmer until chicken is tender, about one hour. Fry peas in remaining butter, add truffles and ham and heat. When serving, place portions of chicken in the center of the plate and surround with the pea mixture. Yield: four servings.

ENSALADA DE NAVIDAD (*Christmas Salad*)

1 cup walnut meats
½ cup almonds, blanched
½ pound cream cheese
½ loaf white bread
1½ cups milk
1 tablespoon vinegar
1 teaspoon salt

½ teaspoon pepper
2 tablespoons olive oil
½ pound tiny onions, boiled
3 large tomatoes, sliced
3 avocados, sliced
3 tablespoons French
    dressing

Grind together nuts, cheese, and bread which has been soaked in milk and drained. Mix well, add vinegar, salt, pepper and olive oil. Place a layer of onions in the salad bowl, cover with a layer of tomatoes and a layer of avocado slices. Add French dressing and cover with walnut and cheese mixture. Yield: six servings.

GELATINA DE NAVIDAD (Christmas Gelatin)

1 pound prunes	1 quart white wine
½ cup sugar	1 cup chopped pecans
1 tablespoon powdered cinnamon	1 cup almonds, toasted and chopped
3 envelopes (tablespoons) gelatin	

Soak the prunes in water to cover for about ten minutes. Cook in the same water with two tablespoons sugar and the cinnamon for twenty to twenty-five minutes or until soft. Pour off liquid, reserving one cup and pit the prunes. Soak the gelatin in reserved juice and then dissolve over heat. Add prunes and the rest of the ingredients. Place in a mold and chill until firm. Yield: about twelve servings.

BOCADO DE DAMA (Lady-Sized Mouthful)

2 cups sugar	2 teaspoons powdered cinnamon
1 cup almonds, blanched and ground	30 lady fingers
½ fresh pineapple	¾ cup grated cheese
9 egg yolks, well beaten	

Boil sugar in one cup of water to 240 degrees F. (a firm ball in cold water). Add almonds. Peel pineapple, remove core, grate and add to almond mixture. Add egg yolks. Simmer over a low flame until the mixture begins to boil, stirring constantly. Add cinnamon.

Spread a layer of lady fingers on a serving platter. Then pour over them a layer of the egg mixture and sprinkle with grated cheese. Repeat layers twice. Serve well chilled. Yield: twelve servings.

CAPIROTADA (*Lenten Pudding*)

Despite official decree and the fact that religion in Mexico was a sub rosa affair until a few years ago, the people of Mexico are passionately Catholic in belief and practice. After a brilliant Mardi Gras preface, they settle down on Ash Wednesday to the forty days of fasting and mourning which traditionally commemorate the period of the Passion of Christ. Fast days are, as in other countries, Wednesday and especially Friday. Capirotada is the Friday Lenten dish and one of the things that makes the Season of Sorrow, as all seasons, a pleasant time to be in Mexico.

1¼ cups brown sugar	⅔ cup any mild cheese,
1½ cups water	grated
2-inch stick cinnamon	½ cup rasins, chopped
10 slices toast, heavily	½ cup pine nuts
buttered	

Mix sugar, water and cinnamon and cook, stirring, until sugar is completely dissolved. Place five slices of toast in a greased pan at least four inches deep. Add half of the syrup, half of the grated cheese, raisins and nuts. Repeat the procedure with the rest of the toast and the remaining ingredients. Bake in a moderate oven (350 degrees F.) about twenty minutes or until mixture has browned. Serve very hot. Yield: six servings.

Chapter 12

Menus

EATING HABITS HAVE CHANGED in Mexico just as in the United States. Twenty or thirty years ago, when people rose earlier, they first had coffee and rolls or fruit and at about 9 o'clock ate a heavy breakfast. In many homes and hotels such breakfast foods as steak with eggs are still typical; in other places visitors to Mexico will be served such gringo fare as corn flakes (pronounced flah-keys) and pancakes. In Mexico City, many eat rather scant breakfasts just as in the United States now. These are typical breakfasts of educated, middle and upper class city dwellers. In the country and particularly in the cattle-raising North, roasted meat or a steak usually accompanies the breakfast.

ALMUERZO TIPICO (*Typical Breakfasts*)

Piña Rebanada o Platanos
(*Sliced Pineapple or Bananas*)

Huevos Ranchero
(*Eggs, Ranch-Style*)

Café con Leche
(*Coffee with Milk*)

———

Fresas
(*Strawberries*)

Frijoles con Chorizo
(*Beans with Mexican Sausage*)

Tortillas o Pan Tostado   Café con Leche
(*Tortillas or Toasted Bread*)   (*Coffee with Milk*)

Jugo de Naranja
(*Orange Juice*)

Tamales de Elote   Chocolate
(*Corn Tamales*)   (*Chocolate*)

———

Papaya
(*Fresh Papaya, always with lime*)

Chilaquiles
(*Poor Man's Dish*)

Frijoles de Olla   Café Negro
(*Beans from the Pot*) .   (*Black Coffee*)

———

Toronja (*Grapefruit*)
Tortilla Mexicana
(*Mexican Omelet*)

Pan Tostado con Azucar   Café con Leche
(*Bread or Rolls, Buttered,*   (*Coffee with Milk*)
Sugared and Toasted)

The main Mexican meal is eaten at midday, which in
Mexico is anywhere from one to three o'clock. Not many
years ago the meals were heavy and included a wet soup,
a dry soup (such as macaroni or rice), a fish course, meat,
invariably a dish of beans, tortillas, bread, coffee—black or
with milk—dessert and fruit. Today people eat more limited
meals. The following dinners are representative of what is
eaten today by most city families. These are menus suitable
for dinner at night in the United States. With all of the
comidas, tortillas are always served and now usually bread
or rolls.

COMIDA (*Midday Dinner*)

Sopa de Pollo
(*Chicken Soup*)

Lengua Almendrada
(*Tongue with Almonds*)

Alcachofas Reina
(*Artichokes, Queen-Style*)
Pan
(*Bread or Rolls*)
Café
(*Coffee*)

Aguacates Rellenos
(*Stuffed Avocados*)
Frijoles Refritos
(*Mexican Fried Beans*)
Mangos
(*Mangoes*)

———

Sopa Toluqueña de Cebolla
(*Onion Soup, Toluca-Style*)
Lomo de Puerco en Cerveza
(*Pork Loin in Beer*)

Papas en Vino
(*Potatoes in Wine*)
Frijoles de Olla
(*Beans from the Pot*)

Ensalada de Rábanos
(*Radish Salad*)
Café
(*Coffee*)

Ante de Almendras
(*Almond Dessert*)

———

Sopa de Albóndigas
(*Soup with Meat Balls*)

Maccarón con Chile
(*Macaroni with Chili*)

Asado (*Roast*)

Timbalitos de Espinacas
(*Spinach Timbales*)
Café
(*Coffee*)

Nabos Guisados
(*Stewed Turnips*)
Guayabas Rellenas
(*Stuffed Guavas*)

———

Sopa de Frijoles
(*Bean Soup*)

Filetes de Pescado a la Tapatía
(*Fish Fillets, Jalisco-Style*)

Arroz Suriano
(*Rice, Southern-Style*)
Tortas de Flor de Calabaza
(*Squash Flower Soufflé*)

Ensalada de Calabacitas y Aguacate
(*Zucchini and Avocado Salad*)

Café   Frutas
(*Coffee*)   (*Fruits*)

———————

MENU FOR AN EXTENSIVE AND TYPICAL MEXICAN DINNER.

Sopa de Carne
(*Meat Soup*)

Arroz Mexicano
(*Mexican Rice*)

Carne en Brazo con Salsa Frita
(*Meat Roll with Fried Sauce*)

Salsifís Empanizados   Enchiladas de Rajas y Queso
(*Breaded Oyster Plant*)   (*Enchiladas Stuffed with
Frijoles Refritos   Pepper Strips and Cheese*)
(*Fried Beans*)   Fruta
Torrejas   (*Fruit*)
(*Cake Slices in Syrup*)   Café Negro
                              (*Black Coffee*)

DINNER MENU FOR A FAST DAY

In Mexico as in other Spanish-influenced countries only
the Fridays in Lent are fast days.

Sopa de Lenteja
(*Lentil Soup*)

Huachinango a la Tampiqueña
(*Red Snapper, Tampico-Style*)

Torta de Papas
(*Potato Soufflé*)

Capirotada   Café
(*Bread Pudding*)   (*Coffee*)
                Cena
              (*Supper*)

Some years ago, it was the custom in Mexico to eat five
times a day. First came early coffee and sweet bread and
fruit, then a heavier breakfast. At about one o'clock, the

234 / Good Food From Mexico

comida was served and at five or six a light merienda, which
would correspond to a substantial tea in England or the
United States. Dinner was served at nine and was usually a
small-scale comida.

Today, however, most Mexicans limit themselves to one
heavy meal which is eaten at midday. The cena and merienda
have been combined and are usually eaten around seven or
eight o'clock.

A typical merienda consists of no more than chocolate
or coffee with sweet buns and fruit, usually stewed. Occasionally one of the antojitos such as tamales is served.
Tortillas are always served for supper.

Enchiladas de Pollo
(*Chicken Enchiladas*)

Pan Dulce
(*Buns and Sweet Breads*)

Café con Leche   Frutas
(*Coffee with Milk*)   (*Fruits*)

———

Sopa de Elote
(*Corn Soup*)

Pan Dulce   Café con Leche
(*Buns and Sweet Breads*)   (*Coffee with Milk*)

———

Tamales de Pollo
(*Chicken Tamales*)

Champurrado   Gelatina
(*Chocolate Atole*)   (*Flavored Gelatin*)

———

Quesadillas
(*Cheese Tortillas*)

Café de Olla   Flan
(*Black Coffee*)   (*Custard*)

BUFFET SUPPER

A typical Mexican menu which might be used for a buffet
supper in the United States.

Caldo
(*Broth*)
Chiles en Nogada
(*Peppers in Nut Sauce*)
Lomo en Avellana, frio
(*Pork Loin in Hazelnut Sauce, cold*)
Ensalada de Verduras
(*Vegetable Salad*)
Chalupitas
(*Little Canoes, hot*)

Chongos Zamoranos   Café or Sangría o Tepache
(*Curds, Zamora-Style*)   (*Coffee, Wine-ade or
                                                 Pineapple Drink*)

Two Mexican customs which might be adapted for parties
in the U. S. are Tamaladas (parties at which nothing is served
but tamales and coffee or chocolate), and the traditional
Christmas Eve custom of eating buñuelos and coffee-with-
milk. The real dinner is not served until after midnight.

Things to Know

Achiote (Anatto). A food coloring obtained from the red waxy substance which coats the spiny fruits of the anatto family, powdered and used to color foods, known in the United States as butter coloring.

Agave (Maguey). Some five species of the century plant are cultivated widely in Mexico as the source of pulque, tequila and mezcal. (The leaves are used for fibre and as "shingling" for the roofs of tiny country houses.) Just before the buds rise from the center of the leaf cluster, a hollow is made with a specially designed knife and the sweet sap is sucked out into a gourd and then emptied into skin bags. After slow fermentation, the sap becomes pulque. Tequila and mezcal are produced by distillation of the ripe pulque.

Aguacate. A native fruit popular since long before the Conquest. The Aztecs called it ahuacatl. There are many varieties of avocado or alligator pear in Mexico and the fruit is eaten in a variety of ways: it is the base for the favorite guacamole; is used as Northerners use butter in sandwiches and also as a garnish. Avocado is a common salad base and sauce ingredient and is eaten alone as a cocktail and quite frequently as an accompaniment for soup.

Aguamiel. Honeywater. Sweet sap extracted from the agave or the maguey cacti which is fermented to make pulque.

Aji. Incan name for hot peppers. The large sweet cool peppers were called chilies, but the Spaniards took over the word chili as a generic title for all of the peppers and the custom of calling even hot peppers chilies persists.

Anatto. See Achiote.

Anizado. Liquor popular in the Isthmus of Tehuantepec.

Antojitos. Diminutive plural of antojo, which means a whim or capricious desire, and consequently has been applied to tidbits like tamales, tostadas, tacos, chalupas, etc.

Ate. Heavy fruit paste frequently served sliced for dessert or as a candy.

Atole. Gruel made of a corn base with the addition of sweetening and various flavorings.

Bizcochos. Biscuits or sweet rolls.

Buñuelos. Large round wafer-thin pastries covered with syrup and served traditionally for fiestas around Christmas and the New Year. Buñuelos are a feature of the Oaxaca festivities where they are sold at sidewalk stands in Oaxaca pottery dishes, which according to custom are smashed when the buñuelos are eaten.

Cacahuate. Peanut, a much-cultivated plant which has been popular since long before the Conquest. The ancient Mexicans called it tlalcacahuatl which means "earth chocolate." Although elsewhere in Latin America called manti, the people of Mexico have retained the old name. Peanuts are widely used in cooking, in sauces, as essential ingredients in desserts and candy.

Cajeta. Thick sauce made of burned milk, somewhat like butterscotch sauce. It is used with crackers or a small portion is served alone. This is a specialty of Celaya.

Camarones. Shrimp, prawns. Cities along the Gulf Coast are famous for shrimp dishes and particularly the state of Campeche, where giant shrimp are found in the coastal waters.

Camote. Sweet potato candy. Sweet potatoes have been cultivated in Mexico for thousands of years. They are eaten as vegetables and used in making the candies called camotes for which Puebla is famous. Sweet potatoes are the base for a number of desserts.

Chayote (Christophine). Large pear-shaped fruit containing a single large seed. It is sold in the United States and cooked like squash.

Chirimoya. One of the fruits of the annona group and related to the custard apple. It has the flavor of vanilla ice cream, is eaten raw and also used in making desserts.

Chicha. Sugar-cane brandy, which is drunk in the Chiapas region, and also a non-alcoholic drink made of chia seeds.

Chicharrones. Mexican equivalent of cracklings, made by rendering lard from fat cut from under the skin of the pig and cooking it until golden brown. Chicharrones are usually served with a chili sauce or with lemon and chili powder.

Chili. The original Nahuatl word for sweet green peppers was chilli. The Spaniards changed the spelling to *chile,* and in turn the English and Americans used *chili.* Although chili was once limited to the green pepper, it is now used as a generic title for all peppers, etc. In Mexico, there is endless variety ranging through all degrees of hotness from the sweet chili ancho to the small hot brown chili piquin. Many varieties are canned. Where these are not available, various peppers found in the United States may be substituted, such as the small red Italian peppers; or chili powder, to taste, with a dash of Tabasco sauce for zest, may be used. In general:

For chile ancho, use bell or green peppers
   chile poblano, use bell or green peppers
   chile pasilla, use green peppers, dried in the sun
   chile serrano, use any variety small red or green hot pepper
   chile Jalapeño, use any variety small red or green hot pepper
   chile verde, use canned green chili pepper
   chile mulato, use any hot pepper

Chilpotle. Variety of chili, rather long and red. It is dried and much used in sauces, when it is diced or powdered.

Chocolate. A pre-Conquest beverage made from the cacao bean. Originally called xoco-atl (sour water) Mexican chocolate has been sweetened by the addition of sugar, cinnamon and other ingredients.

Chongos. Little Knots, one of the two favorite Mexican desserts. It is made from milk boiled slowly and further hardened in a sweet syrup. Several kinds are made, but the most famous are the chongos Zamoranos of Michoacan.

Cilantro. See Culantro.

Culantro or *Cilantro.* Coriander, one of the most widely used seasonings in Mexican cooking.

Enchiladas. Tortillas rolled around chicken, pork or other meats, cheese, beans and other fillings and baked with various sauces.

Frijoles. Beans, especially varieties of kidney beans.

Garnachas. Antojitos made of corn dough, smaller and

thicker than tortillas, and with edges molded up as if for a tiny pie. The center contains any of the quesadilla fillings—cheese, potatoes, or squash flowers. A bit of hot grease is sprinkled over the top and then it is fried in hot fat.

Gorditas. Little Fat Ones, tiny round chunky corn cakes cooked on ungreased skillets. Most famous are the Gorditas de la Guadalupe, sold outside the shrine on feast days.

Granadilla. The fruit of any of the species of passion flowers. Most popular in Mexico is the yellow Granadilla, an oval fruit with a stiff orange rind and a soft jellylike center full of seeds. It is similar in taste and appearance to the maypops of the southern United States.

Guacamole. Salad or sauce made basically of avocado, onion and chili. Frequently chicharrones or tiny bits of crisp bacon and grated hard cheese are added as well as tomatoes, mashed or minced very fine. Guacamole is served on a bed of lettuce as a salad or with fried tortilla wedges as an appetizer, or simply as a sauce.

Guanábana (Soursop). This fruit belongs to the annona family. Several varieties are popular in Mexico: Ilama resembles the custard apple but has a deep pink skin. Manirote has yellow and orange flesh and a strong flavor. Posh-te, a wild variety, has a hard green rind and solid flesh. Guanabana is excellent for conserves and is used to make a delicious ice.

Guayaba (Guava). Grows wild in Mexico and is one of the most popular fruits. Usually oval or rounded, the fruits are small with yellowish skin covering pink granular meat studded with small seeds. Guavas are eaten raw, but are at their best candied or made into the thick fruit pastes called ates.

Horchata. An infusion. Water is allowed to stand for several days with melon seed, coconut or whatever fruit or flavoring is desired. Then it is strained and served cool. A very popular drink for children in Mexico City is oatmeal horchata.

Jalapeño. Variety of chili, rather large, green and pickled entire (with seeds). See Chili.

Jícama. A turniplike root with a subtle apple taste. It is eaten as a raw fruit, and is frequently served with chili powder and a piece of lemon as an accompaniment for tequila drinks. Jícama is also used in salads.

Maguey. Century Plant (see Agave).

Masa. A "dough" made of corn kernels soaked in lime water and ground as fine as possible, masa is all important in the Mexican cuisine since it is made into two primary foods —tortillas and tamales. The basic method of making it involves boiling about three pounds of shelled corn in an equal amount of water to which three ounces of hydrated lime have been added. After the corn is removed from the fire and allowed to cool, it is rubbed between the hands until the skins are loosened and discarded in a cold water rinse. This skinless corn, called Nixtamal, is then ground on a metate very fine. Both Nixtamal and masa may be bought by the pound in Mexican stores. If prepared cornmeal is used, do not use the yellow domestic variety; use white cornmeal.

Metate. Flat slanting stone slab used for grinding corn for tortillas.

Mezcal. Intoxicating drink made by fermenting and distilling the maguey hearts. It is a product of the Oaxaca region.

Molcajete. Stone bowl or pottery mortar with a ridged bottom which is used for grinding chilies, onions, etc.

Mole. Sauce, from the Aztec word molli. There are almost as many moles as there are cooks in Mexico. Dishes frequently take their name from the sauce such as mole de olla which is actually beef stewed in red chili sauce.

Molinillo. Wooden beater used to whip chocolate.

Nixtamal. Corn kernels soaked in lime water for grinding into masa.

Nixtamalina (Tamalina). White corn meal flour. (Very fine and not just the same as corn meal.) In the United States, nixtamalina may be purchased packaged or canned. In Mexico, the finely ground corn meal is bought in damp doughy masses.

Nopal. Prickly pear cactus which bears various colored fruits called tunas, very popular in Mexico. The leaves are used for salad and are combined, cut into thin strips, with eggs to make a Lenten omelet.

Paella. A purely Spanish dish which has been adopted in Mexico. Paella has a rice base and includes as many varieties of sea food as can be procured or are desired. A favorite dish in Mexico.

Papaya. Fruit of a treelike plant grown in Mexico. The popular fruit is large, often weighing ten pounds or more, its flesh ranges from yellow to deep orange, and the center hollow is filled with tiny black seeds. Papaya is eaten chilled with lemon, is made into soft drinks and before it is completely ripe, it is a much-favored base for conserves and dulces.

Pulque. Fermented juice of the century plant.

Quesadilla. Turnovers made of tortillas filled with cheese, potatoes or squash flowers.

Taco (Antojito). Tortilla wrapped around meat, fish, cheese, beans, squash flowers, usually fried in deep fat.

Tamales. One of the most famous and most ancient Mexican dishes, tamales are made of masa spread on a corn husk or—in southern Mexico—on a banana leaf, covered with filling, rolled, tied, and steamed. (Instead of husks or leaves, parchment paper may be used.) Although other Indian cultures enjoyed tamales, the word used today comes from the Aztec language—Nahuatl—tamalli.

Even in Mexico, where time is not the consideration it is north of the border, tamales are regarded as a special dish for festive occasions because of the time required to prepare them. Tamales, searingly hot or bland or very sweet, are best sellers in grocery stores, market stalls, and from five-gallon cans set up by enterprising vendors on street corners in cities and towns.

Tequila. An alcoholic drink distilled from the maguey cactus plant. Both a clear and amber-colored liquid, the latter called tequila añejo, tequila is traditionally served in small cups or glasses, accompanied by a pinch of salt and a piece of Mexican lemon, which resembles our lime. That one-two-three taste sensation helps to keep natives and visitors alike in a gay mood throughout any fiesta.

Torta. Mexican sandwich. A long roll is cut in half, spread with beans. Then a layer of meat is added, shredded lettuce, avocado, cheese and chili.

Tortilla. The basic staple of the Mexican diet, tortillas are made from *masa* patted into small, very thin, round "pancakes" and cooked on a heavy ungreased comal. They are widely sold in the United States today, packaged or canned. Before serving, heat them quickly on a griddle or over a low flame, and bring them to the table wrapped in a clean napkin in a dish so that the heat will not escape. They are torn into smaller pieces or, intact, rolled or folded around foods. They should be stored in the refrigerator and, if necessary, dampened slightly before they are heated at serving time.

Tortillas de harina, flour tortillas, are widely used throughout northern Mexico. They are much larger, although no thicker than tortillas de maíz, and are eaten in the same fashion.

Tostada. An antijito made of a toasted tortilla covered with beans, shredded meat, shredded lettuce, cheese, etc.

Totopo. A small round tortilla fried in hot lard to make it curl and spread with taco mixture. Totopos range in size from a silver dollar to a saucer.

Tuna. The fruit of the prickly pear cactus, tunas come in varying colors and degrees of sweetness. Beneath the stiff rind covered with spines is cool, moist, granular fruit flesh that is delicious plain or served in a salad.

Index

243

Index of Foreign Names

249

IF YOU ENJOYED THESE RECIPES, YOU'LL BE INTERESTED IN THESE OTHER COLLIER BOOKS ON
Cooking

IF YOU ENJOYED READING THIS BOOK, YOU'LL BE INTERESTED IN THESE OTHER COLLIER BOOKS:
Literature